CREATING A LIFE

What Every Woman Needs to Know About Having a Baby and a Career

Sylvia Ann Hewlett

MIRAMAX BOOKS
NEW YORK

Library of Congress Cataloging-in-Publication Data

ISBN: 1-4013-5930-2

First Trade Paperback Edition

10 9 8 7 6 5 4 3 2 1

For my husband Richard with whom I have created a life.

CONTENTS

ACKNOWLEDGMENTS

My greatest debt is to my family—my husband, Richard Weinert, and our children, Shira, Lisa, David, Adam, and Emma. Their generous love has buoyed my spirits and replenished my energies at critical junctures over the last three years.

A special word of thanks is due to the funders of this project. The Center for the Study of Values in Public Life at Harvard University awarded me a fellowship which allowed me to explore the ideas that underpin this book, while Ernst & Young, Merck Inc., the Annie E. Casey Foundation, and the David and Lucile Packard Foundation provided funds that helped underwrite the survey *High-Achieving Women 2001*

and the accompanying research effort which under-
girds chapter 2 of this book. I would also like to thank
Harris Interactive for the efficiency with which they
carried out this survey.

My literary agent, Molly Friedrich, saw this book
through its birth pangs with skill and judgment, while
the "team" at Miramax Books—Tina Brown, Jonathan
Burnham, JillEllyn Riley, Danielle Mattoon, Hilary
Bass, and Kristin Powers lent editorial skill, wise counsel, and unstinting support.

My associates at the Center for Work-Life Policy
and at the School of International and Public Affairs at
Columbia University contributed generous amounts
of time and attention and I thank them. I am especially
grateful to my long time friend and colleague Peggy
Shiller.

I am extremely grateful to the scholars, analysts,
activists, and family friends who so generously shared
their ideas and experience: Enola Aird, Nadine Asin,
Mary Jo Bane, James Barron, Olga Beattie, Chris
Beem, Lisa Belkin, Darel Benaim, Lisa Benenson,
Tessa Blackstone, Ed Blakely, David Blankenhorn,
Raina Sacks Blankenhorn, Rick Bobrow, John
Buehrens, John Mack Carter, Sharon Chantiles, Ellen
Chessler, Susan Chira, Forrest Church, Brent Coffin,
Dan Cohen, Jim Cox, Flora Davidson, Paula Dressel,
John Eatwell, David Elkind, Judy Farrell, Katherine

El Salahi, Tim Ettenheim, Madalina Dumitrescu, Sandy Feldman, Judith Flores, Al Franken, Marc Feigen, Nancy Folbre, Jenny Fielding, Judith Friedlander, Lucy Friedman, Maggie Gallagher, Ellen Galinsky, Mary Ann Glendon, Claudia Goldin, Valerie Grove, Sue Gronewold, Karla Hanson, Lisa Harker, David Harris, Heidi Hartmann, Deborah Epstein Henry, Patricia Hewitt, Jody Heymann, Jean Hewlett, Abby Hirsch, Sarah Holloway, Deborah Holmes, Judith Jadow, Phil Johnston, Enid Jones, Heather Joshi, Bernice Kanner, Helen Knight, Greta Knowles, Dan Kramarsky, Pam Laber, Livia Lam, Jacqueline Leo, Helen Levine, Anne Lonsdale, Katherine Lord, Kathy Lord, Carolyn Buck Luce, Jessye Norman, Linda Mandell, Dana Markow, Bonnie Maslin, Ann Mongovan, Mary Mulvihill, Margaret Munser, Nancy Nienhuis, Sylvia Olarte, Renée O'Leary, Ursula Oppens, Betty Palmer, Sam Peabody, Marina Piccinini, Becky Popenoe, Shari Popkin, Sylvia Poppovic, Chris Powell, Ken Prewitt, Nancy Rankin, Paula Rayman, Sarah Rees, David Richardson, Dick Robinson, Tim Melville Ross, Paul Sacks, Mark Sauer, Diane Sawyer, Juliet Schor, Eleanor Sebastian, Bob Shnayerson, Jim Speros, Maggie Simmons Ruth Spellman, Theda Skocpol, Marilyn Strathern, Jim Steyer, Ellen Stein, Humphrey Taylor, Laurie Taylor, Matthew Taylor, Sarah Thomas-James, Margot Waddell, Jane

Waldfogel, Michael Waldman, Judy Wallerstein, Amy Wallman, Linda Waite, Chris Wasserstein, Thelma Weinert, Dede Welles, Cornel West, Joan Williams, Ira Wolfman, Ruth Wooden, and Marie Young.

Janet Mims, Ed Napier, June Rousso, and Sally Wilson provided invaluable editorial and research assistance, while Norma Vite-León contributed her impressive quantitative and analytical skills. Marthe Abraham, Ada Domenech, Betsy Echevarria, and Andrea Parker played critical roles on the home front. Few authors receive such loyal support and I am extremely appreciative.

Finally, I want to thank the people I interviewed— mostly women but also some men. These interviews give heart and soul to this book. I am particularly grateful to the breakthrough generation women featured in chapter 1 who allowed me to tell their stories so that young women would have a better chance of creating lives that encompass both love and work. I thank them from the bottom of my heart. These stories comprise a rare gift from one generation to the next.

Sylvia Ann Hewlett
New York, N.Y.
December, 2001

PREFACE

You are about to read a book that could change your life.

The facts and figures I assemble on these pages could make a huge difference to your life, your best friend's life, your daughter's life, your sister's life.

Not a week goes by that I don't encounter tangible evidence that *Creating a Life* has shifted attitudes, changed behavior, and transformed individual lives.

Just last week I was boarding the Delta shuttle at Reagan Airport in Washington, D.C. when a thirty-something woman rushed up to me. "Are you Sylvia Ann Hewlett?" I allowed that I was. She let out a yelp of excitement and hugged me fiercely. She then proceeded to tell me—and a random collection of beltway commuters—her story. Just six months earlier she had been a standard issue workaholic—working a sixty-five hour week, pretending that Chinese take-out at her desk was her preferred dining experience. Then her sister sent her my book. She read it, and, as she put it "a light bulb went off in my head." The immediate result: she decided to get out there and take back the reins of her life. In rapid succession she switched companies (to one that encouraged telecommuting, flextime, and had a policy of no e-mails over the weekend), joined a church, an outing club, and met an amazing man. "We're moving in together next month," she told me shyly, "and we're even talking about marriage and children. Your book made such a difference. . . . it gave me clarity and courage."

And last month, after a speech at the Harvard Law School, a student came up to me holding a baby. She introduced herself and then held out the infant. "Here he is," she said, "his name is Nathaniel Patrick, and he's kind of yours. We would not have had him, had it not been for your book." Taken aback—and somewhat shaken—I murmured something supportive and bent over the baby to wipe away a tear or two. Who could fail to be touched?

Dominique—the new mother—then went on to tell her experience. This time last year, she had been one semester into a joint degree program between the

Harvard Law School and Tufts University when she chanced upon my book. Both she and her husband read it—and it transformed their life plan.

Fairly recently married, they had thought that they would wait until she had completed her degrees and launched her career before having a child. In her words, "after reading *Creating a Life* I realized two things: I probably should not wait until my mid-thirties before having that first child because waiting that long would jeopardize my dream of eventually having two to three children. I also realized that it was silly to wait for the 'perfect moment.' It was never 'convenient' to have a child. So I got creative and began to realize that the life of a student is pretty flex-ible. I mean we don't have much money, but neither of us have brutal schedules or overbearing bosses. In important ways it's about as easy as it's going to get."

She looked down at her baby, and, on cue, Nathaniel burped, blinked and let loose on the world one of those totally amazing toothless, infant grins. Dominique beamed. "Isn't he adorable," she said, and we both laughed, it seemed such a gratuitous comment.

Before explaining why *Creating a Life* had this kind of impact on women's lives, I want to go back in time to the spring of 2002, when this book was published in hardcover. The media reaction was quite extraordinary.

The juggernaut started the weekend of April 7th, two days before publication date, when *Time* magazine ran a cover on the book and *60 Minutes* aired a feature. These stories triggered a maelstrom of media attention. The range of the coverage was remarkable. *People* and *New York* magazine ran cover stories but so did the *Harvard Business Review*. News anchors Aaron Brown, Tom Brokaw, and Peter Jennings gave the book major news coverage and I appeared on *Oprah*, *The View*, and the *Today* Show. The coup de grace: in late April *Saturday Night Live* targeted the book, poking fun at both the book and me, confirming the fact that *Creating a Life* had somehow entered the zeitgeist.

By mid-July, I had accumulated close to two thousand clippings. Newspaper articles from cities as far-flung as London, Palm Beach, Sao Paulo, Chicago, Paris, Cambridge, Jerusalem, Sydney, Glasgow, Toronto, and Rome demonstrated that this book had generated a veritable tidal wave of reaction around the world.

Why this huge interest, this vast coverage? What was all the fuss about?

First and foremost women found this book riveting because it gave them the tools—both the information and the can-do attitude—that enable them to get what they want out of life. As Susan Chira pointed out in her *New York Times* review, "fundamentally 'Creating a

Life' is an attempt to help women think about how to get what they want."

The data and the life stories that fill the pages of this book are deeply empowering because they create a "road map" that enables a woman (whether she is twenty-eight or thirty-eight) to make wiser and more deliberate decisions about her life. Cutting edge information on fertility helps a woman understand the real deal on ART and the likelihood of having that miracle baby at the age of forty-two. Even more importantly, powerful new data on career paths and family friendly workplaces help women understand their professional options, which can be surprisingly upbeat. Did you know that close to 30 percent of American employers provide serious support on the work-life balance front—flextime, reduced hour workweeks, job shares, and the like. If you are a woman wanting to create a life that contains both work and family why not seek out an employer that provides these supports? The research shows this can make a tangible difference to a woman's ability to balance career and children. It's trite but true, *KNOWLEDGE IS POWER*. Armed with critical information, women can be smarter and more intentional about both their bodies and their bosses—and thus put themselves in a better position to realize their dreams.

But I'm not just talking about information, I'm also talking about attitudes. At the very beginning of *Creating a Life* I take on this issue directly. How do we combat the mind-set so prevalent in our culture that it is somehow unseemly—or greedy—for women to want it all: love and work, career and children? There is this pernicious idea out there that somehow a woman isn't a woman unless her life is riddled with sacrifice. Remember how Hillary Clinton's approval ratings tanked when she was running the healthcare initiative and soared when she was publicly humiliated by her husband's philanderings!

I can't tell you how many times the professional women I interviewed spoke apologetically about wanting it all. It always made my blood boil. I mean, it isn't as though these women were standing in line waiting for hand-outs. They were quite prepared to shoulder more than their fair share of the work involved in having both career and family. So why on earth shouldn't they feel more entitled and more deserving?

Sure, in real life most women need to compromise at the edges. It's extremely difficult to conjure up either the stamina or the support to maximize achievement in every sphere of life. When I talk about having it all, I don't mean having everything, rather, I mean, having the basics. As I demonstrate, for most women (86 percent to be precise) the basic package boils down to work and family. In the words of Cindy—who is featured in chapter seven:

> "Men are always accusing me of being greedy when I say I want it all. But I'm not talking about the bells and the whistles. I'm talking about the basics: love and work. What sane person doesn't want that? Now maybe if I were shooting to become the CEO of a Fortune 500 company I would expect to have to choose: career or children. But my game plan is to raise two kids and build a part-time career in middle management. Doesn't this sound reasonable?"

Empowerment may have been a dominant theme in the media reaction to *Creating a Life*, but it was not the only theme. Threading through various talk shows and opinion columns was a much more difficult reaction, one which I found extremely hard to deal with because it was laced with serious amounts of pain. The fact is, for some women, *Creating a Life* tapped into a mother lode of anguish and anger. A sub-set of women in their thirties and forties refused to go anywhere near my book because they could not deal with what they imagined was the hurtfulness of my message. They thought that this book would make them feel even more terrible about having missed out on something huge. "I already ache with the loss—those babies I will never have," one forty-three-year-old told me. "Why should I read this book—I need it like a hole in the head."

Because I was able to spend some time with this particular forty-three-year-old, I got to set the record straight. I was able to tell her how this book is full of gutsy, professional women who in their forties and fifties find "food for their souls." One saves an orchestra, another opens an art gallery, and yet another opts to become a single mom—adopting a baby girl from China. I was able to tell her that this book was written to help all of us—whether or not we eventually have children—grow ourselves a life. Among other things *Creating a Life* helps us gird our loins and do battle with a long work-week corporate culture that increasingly hems us in and drains our vital energies.

As I talked to this woman—and others like her—I was newly impressed by what I now see as a "heart of darkness" in our culture. We make it so difficult for successful, professional women to demand both love and work that they find it extraordinarily difficult to own up to their desire for intimacy, companionship, and children. And if you can't admit to needing something, it is extremely hard to get that something! Men wear their need for relationships on their sleeves. Not so women. It somehow exposes their soft underbellies and makes them frighteningly vulnerable.

In the end Carol Gilligan was right. At an event in New York City where she led a discussion of my book, she told an audience that the real significance of *Creating a Life* is that it "breaks a profound silence" enabling women to speak up and tell the world the full range of what they yearn for—and deserve. Most importantly, the book emboldens women by urging them to share experiences and solutions. The passionate and often searing life stories that fill the pages of this book are told by women intent on one agenda: helping their sisters lead real rich multi-dimensional lives. So pick up this book and find out what these courageous women have to say. Whatever your age, whatever your situation, the voices captured in these pages will influence your life, in some way, for the good.

A final word on my action agenda. Much of this book is devoted to solutions—how individual women can take back the reins of their lives, and how government and businesses can create workplaces that are much more flexible and supportive. In my judgment, the single best thing to happen as a result of *Creating a Life* is a modest amount of new traction in the policy arena. In the twelve months since the book came out, a wide spectrum of entities—ranging from Goldman Sachs to Washington and Lee University—have invited me into their organizations to help design a second generation of work-life policies that tackle the long-hours culture head-on. And in September 2002, I was invited to London to help launch Work-Life Balance week in Britain. I used the occasion of my key note address to outline a five-point plan (taken directly from this book) of what the next generation of work-life policies should look like if we want women to have more generous choices in their lives—choices that are at least as good as those faced by men. As I stood on the podium that day at Claridges, looking out at a sea of V.I.P.s—from government, from the private sector, from women's leadership organizations—I realized that *Creating a Life* had delivered in unusual ways. The book hit such a chord and stirred up such a ruckus that it has ended up forcing the establishment to pay attention—and at least toy with the idea of fundamental change. I am deeply grateful.

Sylvia Ann Hewlett
New York, N.Y.
August 2003

PREFACE TO THE
ORIGINAL EDITION

I didn't set out to write this particular book. Indeed, I planned to write something quite different—a book of interviews with women facing 50 at the millennium. My original intention was to create a series of three-dimensional portraits celebrating the achievements of the breakthrough generation—that first generation of women who broke through the barriers and became powerful figures in fields previously dominated by men.

As I began these interviews in the winter of 1998–99,[1] I organized my questions around certain themes: What did these women owe to feminism? Had they leaned on powerful mentors? What strategies did they use to break through the glass ceiling? But as I began meeting with these women those themes got pushed aside as I confronted one remarkable fact: *None of these women had children.* Now, I hadn't chosen to interview Holly Atkinson, Mary Farrell, Judith Friedlander, Charlene Martin, Jessye Norman, Sue Palmer, Lisa Polsky, Diane

Sawyer, Wendy Wasserstein, and Patricia Williams because they were childless; I had simply sought out women who were prominent in a diverse set of fields. It just turned out that all of them were childless. So I went back to ask the obvious: Had these women wanted children? And if they had wanted children, how come they didn't have any?

At first they were guarded, even evasive, in their answers—powerful women with carefully crafted public images do not share their private lives lightly or easily. My questions were cleverly and charmingly deflected. But I found that telling my story—a four-year battle with age-related infertility, a successful pregnancy at age 51—had a magical effect: Stunned silence, delighted laughter, and eager questioning often cleared the way for a much more open and honest conversation.

Once I started to refocus my interviews, another astonishing fact emerged: *None of these women had chosen to be childless.* No one said, "I sat down at age thirty and decided that motherhood was not for me. I planned on devoting my life to building a huge career. I wanted celebrity/power/money—children were an easy trade-off." This is *not* what these women said. Rather, they told haunting stories of children being crowded out of their lives by high-maintenance careers and needy partners. Judy Friedlander, Dean of the Graduate Faculty at New School University, called childlessness "a creeping nonchoice." What she meant was that during her thirties and early forties, career constraints and relationship difficulties gradually squeezed the possibility of having a child out of her life.

I was taken aback by what I heard. Going into these interviews I had assumed that if these accomplished, powerful women were childless, surely they had chosen to be. I was absolutely prepared to understand that the exhilaration and challenge of a megawatt career made it easy to decide not to be a mother. Nothing could be further from the truth. When I talked to these women about children, their sense of loss was palpable. I could see it in their faces, hear it in their voices, and sense it in their words.

In retrospect, I ask myself why I expected these women to have easily given up one of life's great joys: children. After all, men don't. Luciano Pavarotti has a megawatt career, but this does not mean he doesn't have a wife and children. In fact, he has had two wives and two sets of children. So why can't Jessye Norman have the same multidimensional life?

As these interviews unfolded, I uncovered a range of complicated emotions. Some of these women blamed career, some blamed men, many blamed themselves. Some were seriously in pain; others had come to terms with a different kind of life. All wished they had found a way to have children.

Listening to their stories, I was deeply impressed by the unfairness of it all and decided I needed to find out why so many seriously accomplished women face such painful choices on the family front. That is when I changed my book project. That is when *Creating a Life* was born.

Chapter 1 weaves together a series of stories from the front lines. Lawyers, scholars, bankers, journalists, and physicians talk about what it's like to be part of the first generation of what I call "high-achieving women" (see endnote 2-1). Their stories are framed by the voice of playwright Wendy Wasserstein, who has played out the fraught agenda of the breakthrough generation in two dimensions—on the stage and in her own life. In her words: "I tried to make it easier by writing it down. I had Holly, Janie, Heidi, and Judith do it first." As we shall see, despite the fact that Wasserstein got to write it down first, her route was by no means easy. She struggled with age-related infertility like the rest of us, and discovered that having a baby in your late forties can be a monumental challenge.

Chapter 2 relates the vivid stories of chapter 1 to national data—in the United States and elsewhere in the advanced, industrial world. Is this small band of women representative of their generation? The answer is a qualified yes. Some of the women featured in chapter 1 are famous; others have extremely high incomes.

These facts set them apart. But in one crucial respect they are typical of other high-achieving women in the breakthrough generation: a large proportion of them do not have children. These highly accomplished women vaulted over barriers and crashed through glass ceilings, but found it extraordinarily difficult—if not impossible—to have children as well.

Chapter 2 also tells us what is happening in the next generation. Sad to relate, the tough trade-offs faced by middle-aged women dog the footsteps of today's younger women. Indeed, women between the ages of 28 and 40 seem to be having an even harder time balancing career and children than their older sisters.

Of course, not all the women in either generation wanted children. A small percentage of them—approximately 14 percent—chose childlessness. This book is not about these women. My focus is on the millions of women who wanted—but did not or will not—have children.

The bulk of chapter 2 summarizes the existing evidence and presents the results of a new national survey, *High-Achieving Women, 2001,* which I carried out in January 2001.[2] These new data allow me to answer questions such as: How do high-achieving women differ from their male counterparts in terms of work/life balance? Are 35-year-olds doing a better job balancing career and family than 45-year-olds did at that age? Are women entrepreneurs doing better than women on more rigid career tracks? How do high-achieving African-American women compare with white women: are they more or less likely to have both a career and children? Does workplace policy make a difference? When high-achieving women have access to a rich array of work/life options, are they more likely to have both a career and a family?

Chapter 3 tackles what is perhaps the most powerful factor in explaining why so many high-achieving women remain childless: the demands and constraints of what one woman I interviewed described as "high-altitude" careers. Chapter 4 zeros in on the difficulties that accomplished women encounter in the marriage market, and chapter 5 deals with challenges older women face on the fertility front. The plain fact is, if you are a career woman who has had the tenacity to nurture both a career and a long-term loving relationship, you might well be on the wrong side of 35 before you have time to draw breath and contemplate having a child—exactly the point in life when infertility rears its ugly head. Media hype notwithstanding, the new reproductive technologies have not solved fertility problems for forty-something women.

Part I presents the circumstances of today's high-achieving working woman. It shows how the brutal demands of ambitious careers, the asymmetries of male/female relationships, and the difficulties of late-in-life childbearing conspire to crowd out the possibility of having children. This is the "creeping nonchoice" Judy Friedlander talked about.

Part II deals with solutions, and here I present two distinct strategies. First, I advocate attitudinal change and a shift in individual behavior. Young women can take back control—and change the odds—by being much more intentional about their private lives. It's clear from the analysis in Part I that timing is at the heart of the matter. If a high-achieving woman were to make finding a partner a priority in her twenties or early thirties, attaining both career and children would be a much less daunting proposition.

Intentionality is a critical concept, for if ambitious women focus on their careers and leave their private lives on automatic pilot, it is extremely likely that family will be squeezed out. Cathryn Palmieri, 48, managing director of Korn/Ferry International, a leading executive search firm, has an extremely concrete piece of advice for young women: "Ask yourself what you need to be happy at 45. And ask yourself this question early enough so that you have a shot at getting what you want. Learn to be as strategic with your personal life as you are with your career."[3]

Of course, being intentional about marriage and

children would be a whole lot easier if careers were less rigid and less all-consuming. Which brings me to a second set of strategies—those that focus on the workplace.

Over the last 15 years I have been extremely involved in the development of family-friendly work environments. I have designed policies for Fortune 500 companies, for small-scale nonprofits, and for start-up dot-coms. I bring to this book a powerful insight: Professional women who want both a family and a career know that conventional benefits packages no longer cut the mustard. For high-flying women— whether they are business executives, lawyers, physicians, or professors—workweeks have become so long, and competitive pressures have become so fierce, that even a generous package of benefits (which might include flexible hours and childcare subsidies) doesn't begin to address the time crunch in their lives. What high-achieving women need are two things that are not yet readily available: reduced-hour jobs and careers that can be interrupted. As policy analyst Nancy Rankin has pointed out, the career highway as it's currently constructed has all kinds of "off-ramps" but very little in the way of "on-ramps." We need to redefine—or reengineer—this highway so that a professional woman can rejoin her career after having taken significant time out. This would make a great deal of difference to a woman's ability to achieve both career and children.

Does this sound utopian? I think not. In chapter 6 I show that employers are concerned with winning an ongoing war for talent, and are ready to experiment with more radical policies to retain employees. According to Marc Feigen, managing partner of the consulting firm Katzenbach Partners, "despite a somewhat weaker economy, competition for high-quality professional talent remains fierce. People are our number one asset, and recruiting and retaining the very best talent is our number one challenge. Therefore, it is up to us to figure out a new generation of policies that better underpin women's lives."[4] The women who participated in my January 2001 survey had some extremely creative solutions to the time-crunch problem. These are featured in chapters 6 and 7.

Which brings me to a set of personal reflections. Given the subject matter of *Creating a Life,* it is particularly important that the reader know who I am and what I bring to this book in terms of experience and values. This is, after all, a book about how women feel about having children—and not having children. It is hard to imagine more passionate or painful territory. In fact, as I was doing the interviews for this book, I was continually surprised—and humbled—at how raw and near to the surface the emotions are.

And so, in the spirit of full disclosure, I would like to describe how I have wrestled with these issues. It seems only fair to reveal at least as much about my own life as I have asked others to reveal about theirs.

To put it as simply as possible, children have been the most enduring passion of my life. Over a span of twenty-three years, my experience has run the gamut of contemporary motherhood:

- I have given birth to children
- I have lost children
- I have helped raise a stepdaughter
- I have coped with miscarriage and prematurity
- I have battled age-related infertility
- I have dealt with failure as well as success on the career front

As is true for many older mothers, my children were not easily come by. With the exception of Lisa, my oldest child, born when I was 31, none of my children entered this world handily or willingly. From my mid-thirties onward I found it increasingly hard to either conceive or carry a child to term. The births of David, Adam, and Emma were interspersed with the loss of twins, two miscarriages, and age-related infertility. Not coincidentally, these were also years when I was forced out of two careers—as a college professor and as an executive director of a think tank.

As a result of these experiences I bring to the table a deep appreciation of the questions raised by this book. The most difficult challenges of my life have centered on birthing and babies. I understand, in intensely personal ways, how the relentless demands of a career can destroy the possibility of mothering, and how the joys and responsibilities of motherhood can derail an ambitious career. I have lived through many of the trade-offs described in this book; for me they are close-in and personal.

But let's begin at the beginning.

I was raised with five sisters in a narrow-minded, unemployment-ridden mining community in South Wales. The landscape of my childhood was littered with reminders of an oppressive past. In the 1950s the "valleys" looked like a film set for the industrial revolution. I remember going on walks with my grandfather and looking with round-eyed wonder at the shuttered collieries, abandoned slag heaps, and row upon row of ramshackle terrace houses straggling up the hillsides. Even the omnipresent sheep were dirty and decrepit, their woolen coats clogged with the same coal dust that clung to my skin and clothes. When I was a teenager, there was a drastic round of pit closures; many of the remaining mines and steel mills shut down and unemployment shot up to the 20 percent level.

My father was a schoolteacher and a charismatic, unconventional man. Once he had adjusted to the fact that there was to be no son—and I remember him being appalled when his 45-year-old wife gave birth to a sixth girl—he set about guiding and shaping his daughters. "Marriage is no solution to your lives," we were told with broken-record repetition from our earliest years. My dad simply didn't want his girls to marry an unemployed miner or work in Woolworth's. He had feminist instincts before they were fashionable and told us with enormous force and clarity that we had to get ourselves an education and find our own way in life.

When I was 13, my father took me to visit Cambridge University. He showed me its ethereal beauty and told me that if I worked hard enough and set my sights high enough I could gain admission and transform my life. Looking back, I am amazed at the audacity of his ambition. Why did my father believe that I could make it into this elite university? I was, after all, a child who spoke English with a thick working-class accent, and who attended a school that in eighty years had never sent a student to Cambridge.

Wherever my father's confidence and courage came from, it rubbed off on me. I set my sights on Cambridge and got down to the hard, grinding work of preparing for the entrance examinations. Four years later I did squeak in, and true to my father's promise, a Cambridge education did enormously expand what I could do with my life.

I did well at Cambridge and after graduation won a Kennedy Scholarship to Harvard University. I went on to complete a Ph.D. in economics. In 1974 I decided to make my home in America and accepted a job as assistant professor of Economics at Barnard College, Columbia University. Two years later I married Richard Weinert, a businessperson in his mid-thirties who already had a child by a first marriage. It is only with hindsight that I realize just how lucky I was to fall in love with this dear man. I cannot claim to have been particularly prescient. When we first met, all I knew was that I was captivated by Richard's joyful energy, his keen intelligence, and huge appetite for life. What I didn't give a whole lot of thought to at the time was whether this ambitious scholar-turned-entrepreneur would mature into the kind of man who would give pride of place to family. But miraculously he did. Over the decades we have spent together he has devoted a huge chunk of his imaginative intelligence to supporting and celebrating his wonderful—if demanding—children and his high-maintenance wife.

But to return to my story. In 1977, Richard and I had our first baby together. Lisa was an extremely wanted child, and we were profoundly happy to have a beautiful, healthy daughter. The first few months of her life, however, turned out to be unexpectedly difficult. For starters, Barnard College offered no parenting leave (paid or unpaid). I had to be back at work ten days after giving birth, and the first magical weeks of Lisa's life were swallowed up in a fog of exhaustion. More serious challenges were to follow.

Two years later I lost twins in the sixth month of pregnancy. This miscarriage occurred, quite literally, "on the job." I was sitting in my office in a state of utter exhaustion after a ten-hour workday when liquid began to trickle down my legs. Befuddled, at first I didn't know what was going on. Then, as the trickle turned into a stream, I realized with horror that my waters had broken and that it was much too early to go into labor—I was only 23 weeks pregnant. By then my boots were filled with liquid and a great puddle was spreading across my office rug. I stumbled out into the corridor, and upon discovering that I was alone in the building, made my way dripping, shivering, and sobbing across the cold, dark campus to Broadway. I hailed a cab and asked to be taken to Lenox Hill Hospital.

Hours later, a grim-faced obstetrician told me that if my body did not go into contractions and if the amniotic fluid replenished itself, I had a very small chance of saving the babies. The more probable outcome was that over the course of the next 48 hours I would spontaneously go into labor and the babies would be born. Given their estimated size (approximately one pound each), they would have no chance of survival.

I spent two days in limbo, lying flat on a hard hospital bed, sick with fear and praying to some ill-defined deity for the lives of my children. Then the doctors did a sonogram and found that not only were the babies alive, but they were floating around in what seemed like plenty of amniotic fluid. I was overjoyed. But on the morning of the third day I awoke to find something strange and hard protruding from my vagina. It was an umbilical chord and it was lifeless. No blood pulsed through the lifeline to the baby; it was stiff and dry like a withered stalk. One of the children was dead. I frantically rang for a nurse, and then everything started happening at once. Nurses, doctors, and stretchers arrived and I was rushed to the delivery floor. "What are you doing?" I cried "The other baby is still alive." One of the doctors patiently explained that they had no option but to induce labor. There was a dead baby in my uterus and I was in danger of developing a life-threatening infection. Both babies had to be delivered. One was dead; the other would die. I hit my head against the steel railing of my bed and told them not to touch me. It was Richard who finally persuaded me that I had no choice. We could have more babies, he said, but there was only one of me.

Later that morning I started a "normal" fourteen-hour labor. I screwed up my eyes and plugged my ears so that I would not see or hear my dead and dying babies being born, but I felt them, warm and wet against my thighs. Although my obstetrician claimed that a natural (i.e., undrugged) labor was quicker and safer, to my dying day I will never understand why he couldn't or wouldn't knock me out with anesthesia to spare me such gratuitous agony.

Afterward, for quite a long time, life was truly hard to bear. My breasts swelled up hard and hurtful, full of milk for my dead babies. Several weeks later my breasts were still leaking milk, a constant reminder of my loss. But I needed no reminder. I mourned my children with an intensity that frightened me. In addition to my cruel grief, I was ridden with guilt. If only I had taken time off from work. If only I had had the guts to risk my career. I felt I had failed to protect my babies and therefore had no pity on myself.

Ironically, I also lost my job. Eighteen months after losing the twins, I was turned down for tenure at Barnard and was forced to step down from a job I both loved and felt I had sacrificed a great deal for. Despite a stellar record, the Ad Hoc Committee at Columbia University denied me tenure because I was not sufficiently committed. In the words of one committee member, I had "allowed childbearing to dilute my focus." I found myself wishing I had been a Barnard faculty member in the 1930s, when the Dean of the College, Virginia Gildersleeve, had a deeper appreciation of the value of a balanced life. In 1937 she wrote, "Neither the men nor the women on our staff should be forced into celibacy, and cut off from that great source of experience, joy, sorrow and wisdom which marriage and parenthood offer."

Two years later Richard and I had a healthy second child, and gradually the dreadful sense of failure ebbed away. But the dark winter of 1979–1980 permanently changed my priorities and my perspective. I was newly appreciative of the fact that the needs of children often run full tilt into adult agendas.

The death of the twins also put me in touch with the far-reaching importance of policies that support working parents. If I had been able to take some "parenting leave," those babies might well have survived. But at that time Barnard College had no family-friendly policies. This flagship of feminism simply didn't see a need for them. Indeed, my various attempts to organize a committee to press for parenting leave were beaten back; such initiatives smacked of special privilege in an era when newly liberated professional women were supposed to be "cloning the male competitive model."

On a more personal front, the death of those children

left a gaping void that I spent years trying to fill. I'm sure that this loss was one powerful reason why Richard and I went on to have several more children.

During my thirties I was not only pushed off a career track, I was also forced to take myself off-track. After leaving Barnard I became executive director of the Economic Policy Council—a private-sector think tank composed of 100 business and labor leaders who deliberated on the outstanding policy issues of the day. Although I had negotiated a slightly reduced work-week, by 1985 it was clear to me that the mounting pressures of this high-profile job were beginning to crowd out the legitimate demands of my then small children. I was becoming a burned-out, tuned-out wife and mother. How could I help my five-year-old deal with separation anxiety when I needed to catch the 7:30 A.M. shuttle to Washington two out of his first three days in kindergarten? I was spread too thin; something had to go. So I quit my job. One day I just walked in and resigned this glamorous plum of a job. At the time I tried to focus on the positives. After all, I had options. My husband earned a good living, so I did not need to maximize my earnings. Besides which, I was fortunate to have a viable alternative: I could build on the success of my last book and write at home, a career much more compatible with family life. Still, there was a painful undertow of regret.

I resigned the week of my thirty-ninth birthday, and as I moved out of my corner office on East 42nd Street, I knew that I was shooting myself in the foot, that this was the end of my "male," on-track career. Even if I managed to become a successful freelance writer, I would never again be seen as an up-and-coming hot-shot, a contender for the big bucks or the impressive title. But I knew what I had to do. I went home, regrouped, and started a new career as an author and activist. I worked odd hours, traveled only rarely, and saw a great deal of my kids.

During those years at home in my early forties I remember becoming quite obsessed with the notion that I might "turn into my mother"— a talented artist and teacher whose independent ambitions were oblit-erated by children. From age 26, when she had her first child, until age 56, when her sixth and last child entered secondary school, my mother barely had time to take a bath, let alone do anything more substantial for herself. Her trek to and from primary school stands out in my memory with particular clarity.

When I was about nine, my family moved to a home on a heavily trafficked main road. The elementary school we children attended was about a mile away, and the route to school involved crossing several busy and somewhat dangerous roads. These were the days before crossing guards, school buses, or school lunches, and my family did not own a car. So four times a day my mum walked us to and from school: at 8:45 A.M. and 12:15 P.M., and again at 1:30 P.M. and 3:15 P.M. Eight times a day she made this trip on foot, pushing the youngest child in a stroller.

Looking back, I am staggered by the relentless and oppressive rhythm. How did my mother find the time to clean, shop, and cook, let alone paint or draw? And all that walking can't have been much fun; sheets of cold, driving Welsh rain often accompanied her on those treks to and from school. Several times a week we all arrived home with wet socks and chattering teeth. And yet my mother was for the most part cheerful and good-humored. At 12:15 P.M. and at 3:15 P.M. she always seemed pleased to see us. We used to run up to her, eager to share a drawing or a piece of inconse-quential school news. When I was eleven I left this pri-mary school and moved on to grammar school, but four younger sisters remained in the pipeline. My mum made these trips for an additional 12 years.

Back in 1843, Elizabeth Cady Stanton told a reporter, "Put it down in capital letters: SELF-DEVELOPMENT IS A HIGHER DUTY THAN SELF-SACRIFICE." What better example of mater-nal self-sacrifice than my mother's trek to and from primary school? And as a mother raising three young children, it scared me silly. I have always thought that one of the most valuable contributions of feminism is that it has enabled women to consider it moral to care not only for others, but also for themselves. Not that this feminist insight totally solves the problem. For most of us, getting the balance right between self and others is a tricky business.

For me, getting the balance right translated into a fierce determination to hang on to my professional identity. Although I was based at home and available to my children for large chunks of the day, I worked extraordinarily hard at preserving enough time for writing. At night I regularly "stole" two hours between 12:00 and 2:00 A.M. I learned to write in taxicabs and buses, and taught myself to concentrate while *Clifford the Big Red Dog* played in the background.

As a result of these stratagems, in the late 1980s and early 1990s I wrote a series of books about women, children, and public policy—*A Lesser Life, When the Bough Breaks,* and *Child Neglect in Rich Nations*— which gave me a voice in the public debate about how to better support American families. To my great delight, I was increasingly invited to help shape policy both in the private sector and in government.

The very success of this second, more flexible career gave me the courage to pursue a long-standing dream—to have one more baby before it was too late. I was thoroughly aware of how hard this would be. By this stage I was in my mid-forties and coping with age-related infertility. I was also contending with a husband who had a hard time understanding why I wanted this late-in-life baby. In early 1993, after a lengthy soul-searching process, I finally persuaded him to come on board for this project. We then spent close to four years pursuing increasingly difficult options, which escalated from egg-stimulating Clomid pills, to daily injections of Pergonal, to cutting-edge versions of IVF. Simultaneously, we pursued adoption possibilities in Texas and California (states which seem to have cornered the market on unwanted Hispanic babies). Thus, I know what it feels like to be a premenopausal woman yearning for that one last baby, engaged in a desperate race against time. As the months rolled into years, I knew I was running out of eggs and hitting age ceilings. Infertility clinics and adoption agencies were beginning to shut me out. (Most IVF clinics won't accept women over 45— they're seen as bad for business because they bring success rates down.)

In the end, Richard and I won this high-stakes, high-tech battle. In the summer of 1996 one embryo was finally persuaded to adhere to my womb, and over the course of eight months little Emma grew big enough to be born. On March 17, 1997, I gave birth just after my 51st birthday. I am deeply appreciative of how lucky we are. I know full well that only a tiny percentage of women who attempt IVF after age 40 actually achieve a live birth.

Given this history I believe I have a special understanding of the unfathomable—and unfashionable—depths of the drive to have children. This thing has a terrible power. If you're over 40, the desire to have a baby before it's too late can kick in with ferocious intensity. It can become a nonnegotiable demand—a veritable obsession—that rides roughshod over every other aspect of life.

All of this must be hardwired. It isn't as though we get much support or encouragement from the culture these days. Try explaining to an ambitious young colleague why you want a baby: for the thrill of being sidetracked in your career? For the right to change dirty diapers and deal with the 2:00 A.M. feed? For the experience of shelling out half a million dollars in school tuition? When Emma was born, my professional peers were particularly uncomprehending and censorious because I already had older children. What could this woman be thinking? Was I neurotic, delusional, or merely frustrated in my marriage or my career? I sometimes found myself in the cowardly position of allowing colleagues to assume that Emma was some kind of surprise. I just woke up on my fiftieth birthday and discovered that I was pregnant! This preposterous notion seemed easier for them to accept than the true explanation—that I adore children and find motherhood extraordinarily fulfilling.

It's hard to talk about my love for my children. It's so easy to sound corny, smug, or just plain self-congratulatory. But I mean to try—by telling a small story that I think captures one of those glorious gifts children confer on their parents.

A few years back Richard and I attended High Holy Day services at B'nai Jeshurun, a synagogue on the Upper West Side of Manhattan. (Richard is Jewish, I am not.) On that particular holiday the senior rabbi told a story:

Many centuries ago there lived a holy man who delighted in his God and devoted a good part of every day to prayer. But the circumstances of his life changed. His community fell on hard times and needed to make many more demands on him. He found, to his dismay, that he was increasingly caught up in worldly pursuits, that his days were filled with noise and clamor. So this wise man devised a plan. He hired an assistant and gave him one very important task. He asked this young man to follow him around, shadowing his footsteps, and on the hour, every hour, to tap him on the shoulder, look him in the eyes, and remind him that there was a God. Sure enough,

over time, the Holy man was able to push aside
the pressures of the world and reclaim his connec-
tion to God.

In my life I often feel that my children play the role of
the Holy man's assistant, constantly reminding me of
what is really important, and thus enabling me to keep
the clamor of the world at bay. When my three-year-old
tugs at my skirt and plaintively tells me that she *has* to
go and feed the ducks *now,* or when my 23-year-old e-
mails me with some urgent, agonized, existential question, it becomes relatively easy to defer or adjust some
professional commitment.

Obviously there are some exceptional individuals
who are able to reach for the sublime by making music,
painting pictures—or playing baseball. But for ordi-
nary mortals like myself, it's often a child who helps us
"touch the face of God."

And in our market-driven existences we need that—
most desperately. Nothing drove this point home more
powerfully than the terrible events of September 11,
2001. The awful carnage of that morning convinced
many of us that our lives were filled with a great deal of
noise and clamor, signifying . . . rather little. We were
forced to reflect that we live in a society in which market work, driven by competition, profits, and greed,
increasingly crowds out nonmarket work, driven by
commitment and care. And in the aftermath of the

tragedy we have become newly committed to our loved ones, newly determined to ask "what's of value, what's core."[5] In a post–September 11 world we may be able to better appreciate how much we need our children.

So there we have it. This is part of what I bring to this book—passionate, painful, and intimate detail grounded in my more than twenty years of experience as a mother. In writing this book I found that this personal dimension was enormously important. More than anything else it helped me establish a bond with the women I interviewed. Sharing my own stories of love and loss, tenderness and tension, made it difficult for others to avoid or deny the difficult questions I flung their way.

A final word. Most of us women who have struggled to find balance in our lives know that there is no simple way to have it all. Risk and compromise mark our everyday experience, even when we are reaching for—and grasping—all that is new and glorious in women's lives.

I will never forget that chalkboard, high up and prominent in the nurses' station. It was 4:30 on the afternoon of March 17, 1997—the date and time are emblazoned in my mind—and I was being wheeled onto the labor and delivery floor of Presbyterian Hospital in Manhattan for an emergency C-section.

I was nervous and jittery, yet I couldn't help but

read this chalkboard. It displayed data on patients newly admitted to the ward: gestational age of baby, age of mother, duration of labor, etc. I checked out my numbers. Some were quite standard. At 36 weeks, my baby was officially full-term, a medical nonevent. Then came the nonstandard piece of information—age of mother: 51. This was particularly eye-popping given that the mother listed above me was 17 years old and the one listed below me was 28. A good 20 years separated me from the next oldest patient on the floor.

I remember feeling thoroughly mortified. I had just been told that my precious, high-tech baby was in a dangerous position—her left foot was sticking down the birth canal and the umbilical chord had prolapsed. The doctors were reassuring, but I was worried sick. Would they get her out in time? Had she been damaged? In my overwrought state the last thing I wanted was to be stared at or otherwise scrutinized. I mean, what a time to feel like an exhibit in a freak show! I remember pulling my pale green surgical cap over my face to hide my tears—and my identity.

But 24 hours later, with my beautiful baby safely born, I was better able to deal with the instant celebrity that came with the chalkboard. News that a 51-year-old had just given birth to a healthy baby spread like wildfire through this New York teaching hospital, which seemed to have more than its fair share of professional women coping with urgently ticking biological clocks. During my six-day postpartum stay—both Emma and I were in pretty bad shape after the caesarean—I had a steady stream of visitors: physicians, nurses, radiologists, social workers. Most were women in their forties, eager for good news on the child bearing front, wanting to reach out and touch someone who had so clearly defied the odds. They treated me as though I had personally extended the number of years they had left to bear children. Their willingness to celebrate with me, to marvel at my brand new baby, to find the right balm for my cracked nipples and vases for my flowers, made me cry. And it wasn't just raging post partum hormones. As I counted Emma's toes and fingers and gave fervent and humble thanks for my great good fortune, I hoped against hope that they too could defy the odds and find a way to have babies.

PART I

CHALLENGES

I

STORIES FROM THE

FRONT LINES

*T*HERE IS A SECRET OUT THERE, A painful, well-kept secret: At mid-life, between a third and half of all high-achieving women in America do not have children.[1] A nationwide survey of high-earning career women conducted in January 2001 shows that 33 percent of them are childless at ages 40–55, a figure that rises to 42 percent in corporate America.[2] By and large, these high-achieving women have not chosen to be childless. The vast majority yearn for children. Indeed, many have gone to the ends of the earth to find a baby, expending huge amounts of time, energy, and money. They subject themselves to humiliating medical procedures, shell out tens of thousands of dollars, and derail their careers. Mostly to no avail. After age 40 only 3 to 5 percent of those who use the new assisted reproductive technologies (IVF and the like) actually succeed in having a child—no matter how much they spend, no matter how hard they try.

Why has the age-old business of having babies become so very difficult for today's high-achieving women? They are better educated, command higher salaries, and enjoy greater access to careers than any generation of women before them. In addition they have longer life spans and many more reproductive options. Yet all of this new status and power has not translated into better choices on the family front— indeed, when it comes to children, their options seem to be a good deal worse than before. Woman can be play- wrights, presidential candidates, and CEOs, but increasingly, they cannot be mothers.

We will begin to learn how and why this has hap- pened by sharing the stories of nine high-achieving women from the breakthrough generation. Wendy Wasserstein, Stella Parsons, and the other women fea- tured in this chapter grew to maturity on the crest of the women's movement, fought hard to succeed in careers their mothers could only have dreamt of, and realized—in many cases too late—that among the sac- rifices they were expected to make were . . . children. For them, combining career with family has been a seriously difficult if not impossible challenge. Now in their mid- and late forties, with their childbearing years essentially behind them, they invite us into their lives to share their struggles. Their stories offer insight and understanding and provide valuable information. It behooves the next generation to pay attention. By doing so, twenty-something women might be able to avoid the cruel choices that dogged the footsteps of their older sisters.

I don't want to suggest that young women are thoughtless or naive. They know it's rough out there. When they look at the senior women in their organizations they cannot help but notice that rather few of them have rich family lives, that many seem isolated and lonely. My concern is that many of today's young women seem convinced that their circumstances—and choices—are vastly improved. They believe that employers these days are more accommodating, that men are more supportive, and that women can rely on getting pregnant deep into their forties. As one 29-year-old woman lawyer told me, "the pioneer women of the '70s and '80s paid some kind of special price for their careers. For us, things are different. We plan on having it all."

But is such easy confidence warranted?

I think not.

As we shall discover in chapter 2, women in their

twenties and thirties are dealing with the same cruel trade-offs. Indeed, if anything, these trade-offs are deeper and fiercer than ever. To pretend otherwise, to imagine that somehow these dreadful choices have gone away, merely covers up and obscures the real challenges.

Thus, the voices from the breakthrough generation must be heard; young women have much to learn from their stories. The plotline of these lives is important: what worked, what went wrong. But the emotional arc is crucial as well. It is profoundly important to understand what these women now regret, and what they glory in.

Let's begin with Wendy Wasserstein—a woman who after a ten-year struggle finally did get a child in under the wire. In all kinds of ways Wendy was one of the lucky ones. In September 1999 Liz Smith broke the happy news in *Newsday*.

> One of Broadway's most gifted playwrights and New Yorker par excellence has had a baby girl at Mt. Sinai Hospital. The baby was most welcome since Wendy had been yearning for motherhood for eons, but the infant was premature so she will be hospitalized for a little while. (The father's name has not been announced.) Congratulations, dear Wendy. You did it your way.

The Liz Smith piece put a brave face on a difficult reality. Wasserstein had developed an age-related medical condition that triggered an emergency caesarean in the sixth month of her pregnancy, so Lucy Jane was born three months premature and had to stay in the hospital for the first ten weeks of her life. The enormous emotional and practical challenges then facing Wasserstein were compounded by the fact that there was no father to share the wrenching trauma of having a child in neonatal intensive care. But hey, no one promised it would be easy having a child at age 48.

The New York Times has called Wasserstein "the voice of the breakthrough generation"[3] for the very simple reason that the triumphs and tribulations of this extraordinary cohort of women thread through Wasserstein's work as well as her life. These women reaped the benefits of the equal rights legislation of the 1960s and 1970s, which dramatically increased the range of opportunities available to them. On the career front the news was nearly all good—barriers were knocked down, and for the first time women could attend Yale University, play soccer, and take out a mortgage. In their private lives, too, they found themselves in uncharted territory, and here the results have been decidedly mixed.

Wasserstein is a woman thoroughly in touch with

the opportunities wrought by modern feminism. In an interview in January 1999 (just before she finally succeeded in getting pregnant), she was emphatic on the subject: "I think the women's movement saved my life. In fact, I know it saved my life.

> My mother sent me to Mt. Holyoke because someone told her "Smith is to bed, Holyoke is to wed." And had I gone to Mt. Holyoke in the 1950s I would surely have gotten wed and ended up as a housewife in Scarsdale. A whole part of me—the creative part—would have died. But suddenly this thing showed up which expanded possibilities. The women's movement gave me the right to find my own voice—and the belief that my own voice was worth finding. It's extraordinary—that an idea can do this for someone.

Yet for Wasserstein, the women's movement did little to help with that other set of goals that revolve around marriage and children.

> For me the reproductive thing has been huge. I mean, if I were a man I would decide at this point to marry some attractive, accomplished 34-year-old woman who wanted children and was willing to put her career on hold to raise our kids. Maybe I would have to take on an extra job writing movies to support us. But I could do that. No problem.

Instead of this standard, male scenario, I have just spent seven years trying to have a child on my own. I started off low-tech with two years of Pergonal. When this didn't work I moved into high-tech reproductive territory. Over five years I did GIFT (gamete intrafallopian tube transfer), seven cycles of IVF, and even tried surrogacy. A woman named Marcy flew in from Alaska to be implanted with embryos created out of my eggs and some donated sperm. But the whole effort didn't pan out. Somewhere along the line the embryos deteriorated—in packing or storage— and were unusable. Marcy went back to Alaska.

By this point I've gone through so many proce- dures—and been injected with so many drugs—I can't even keep track of them all. What did I get out of all this? All I've proved is that I can't get pregnant, that I'm really not a girl.

At first I thought I was up for anything. You show up, the doctor shows you a range of high- tech options, and there's this powerful thing—the promise of a child. But before you know it you've flunked the third year running and you're begin- ning to feel used and abused—not to mention broke. You sit in clinics that are wallpapered with pictures of babies, but despite the fact you try as hard as you know how, you don't get to have one of those babies.

I'm no longer sure that this technology is

38   CREATING A LIFE

remotely empowering. You take a woman of my
generation, someone who is seriously accomplished, but is in her forties and hasn't had a
child. This new technology becomes a way of
telling her that whatever she accomplished, it
isn't enough. And then when she fails to get
pregnant—and most of us do fail—it erases her
sense of professional competence and erases her
confidence as a woman. I know these procedures
left me feeling more depressed than at any other
time in my life.[4]

There is more than a hint of bitterness here. I haven't
talked to Wasserstein since her successful pregnancy,
which obviously transformed what she feels about ART,
but back in the winter of 1999, she was hugely resentful
about what these technologies had done to her life.

"Why is the nasty, painful stuff around sex and
reproduction always dealt with by women?" she railed.

There were IUDs when I was in college and now
they are injecting us with God knows what. Why
is it never the men? Or at least when
it involves men it's Viagra—something potent and
pleasurable.
    It can be frightening, this yearning for a child—
it's hard to fathom the desperate urgency. And I
guess I haven't given up. I mean, I still have these
adoption lawyers calling me, and I'm thinking of

having one more stab at IVF. For me, coming to
terms with this thing might mean battling on until
I actually have a child.[5]

Hesitant, defiant, her voice trailed off. Two months
later, this remarkable and valiant woman became pregnant with little Lucy.

So there we have it: a Pulitzer Prize–winning playwright, one of the most admired women of my generation, helplessly mired in a struggle to have a
baby—her enormous accomplishment irrelevant to the
task at hand. Indeed, as I discovered in many hours of
conversation with Wendy Wasserstein, these very
accomplishments hindered her ability to have a family.
Over the years, her considerable success has been
immensely threatening to men. One long-term
boyfriend, for example, threatened to break up their
relationship if her play *Uncommon Women* moved to
Broadway. The play made it and the boyfriend walked
out. When she turned 40, Wasserstein finally gave up
on finding Mr. Right and began seriously trying to
have a child on her own. It was then that she ran full
tilt into another set of problems—problems that centered on her own declining fertility.

Nowadays, the rule of thumb seems to be that the
more successful the woman, the less likely it is she will
find a husband or bear a child. For men the reverse is
true. The more successful the man, the more likely he

is to be married with children. One pair of figures from corporate America says it all: 49 percent of women executives earning $100,000 or more a year are childless, while only 19 percent of 40-year-old male executives in an equivalent earnings bracket do not have children.[6]

This glaring gap between the ability of high-achieving men and women to have children is underscored by the Wasserstein family itself. The very week Wendy Wasserstein was dealing with preeclampsia and the premature birth of baby Lucy, her sister-in-law was settling in across the hallway at Mt. Sinai Hospital. Claude Wasserstein, 34, wife of Wendy's brother, Bruce, was at the hospital for the birth of their second child. Claude is Bruce Wasserstein's second wife, and the bouncing eight-pound baby boy she delivered in September 21, 1999, is Bruce's fifth child. As with so many men, fame and fortune for Bruce Wasserstein— an exceptionally successful investment banker—has been accompanied by beautiful wives and many children. This happy coincidence of fame and family did not materialize for his equally successful sister, Wendy. Nor does it for most high-achieving women.

Of course, in the end Wasserstein did have a baby, and early one Sunday morning in September 2000 she talked about her miraculous journey. She was back at Mt. Sinai Hospital giving the opening address at the annual RESOLVE conference—RESOLVE is a nationwide organization that provides information and support to those dealing with infertility. Attending the conference were over five hundred people—couples and single women—all in the throes of infertility treatment. Wasserstein took this opportunity to explain how she finally got her child.

"After seven years of failure I thought I had quit trying," she said. Then, at a restaurant, she ran into one of her first fertility doctors, who told her that new technology would give her a 50/50 chance for a child. Six months later she was pregnant, facing an entirely new set of challenges.

In her sixth month Wasserstein was diagnosed with preeclampsia. She was hospitalized and the pregnancy stabilized, but sixteen days later her condition suddenly deteriorated and the doctors decided to deliver the baby by caesarean section. On the afternoon of September 12 Lucy Jane was born, 14 inches long and weighing 790 grams, or one pound, 12 ounces.

Wasserstein described the first time she held her daughter. "Lucy Jane was almost weightless. Her tiny legs dangled like a doll's. Her diaper was the size of a cigarette pack."

During Lucy's stay in the hospital, Wasserstein experienced some heart-stopping moments. The evening of Yom Kippur, the holiest day of the Jewish year, she arrived back at the hospital and found that Lucy had needed a blood transfusion and now had a respirator tube taped over her nose and mouth. Another time she arrived and noticed that Lucy's tiny knit cap had been cut down the center.

Wasserstein panicked and ran down the corridor in search of a doctor. It turned out they had taken another brain sonogram; Lucy's brain ventricles were enlarged and needed to be monitored.

But pint-size Lucy Jane had an iron constitution. Not only did she take these medical crises in stride, she grew and she flourished. Ten weeks after birth she was allowed to go home.

Wasserstein finished her Sunday morning talk at Mt. Sinai on an emotional note.

"Lucy Jane is one year old this week. And she is thriving. That is the first miracle," she said. "The fact that I was able to make the choice to have this baby—that it was medically possible, that it was culturally possible—that is the second miracle."

I looked around the Stern Auditorium. There was hardly a dry eye in the room.

Later that morning I met up with Stella Parsons, 45. Stella and I are old friends—back in 1991 we had been part of the same Clinton transition team. She was in town for the RESOLVE conference and we had arranged to meet. We sat in a corridor at Mt. Sinai, nursing our coffee, trying to figure out which session of the conference we wanted to go to next. Stella was still reeling from the emotions triggered by hearing Wasserstein talk.

"It's not that she was trying to be offensive or anything—she was funny, poignant, and gutsy, just like those wonderful women in her plays—but she might have said more about failure and loss. I mean, she was talking to a roomful of women who either haven't gotten pregnant, or who have gotten pregnant and lost a kid or two. And there she was," said Stella, clearly getting agitated, "a fucking walking miracle. Not only did she get pregnant at age 48, but her 1 lb., 12 oz. baby survived, and by all accounts, is flourishing. I don't know how to wrap my mind around her good fortune. It just doesn't square with my reality."

I waited quietly. Stella was dumping sugar in her coffee and clearly had more to say. "A huge part of it is money, and that makes me angry. Here's a woman who's spent a ton of money on a baby. If you just add up the stuff she's talked about—seven IVF attempts, two failed attempts at using a surrogate mother—you get to $130,000. What kind of a model is that for real people? John and I had to take out a second mortgage for our three attempts at IVF. And what a joke that was! Not only did all three fail, but they so depleted our financial reserves, we had to pinch and scrape for two whole years before we could think about trying again.

I know that Wasserstein went through a shitload of stuff, but she doesn't know what it feels like to be 43 with a biological clock that's ticking like a time bomb, and to be forced to sit tight and do nothing because you can't afford to." Stella's voice was high and harsh.

Stella and I got together two days later for a long, leisurely lunch. The big news was that she had just been offered a chair at Ohio State University. I started to congratulate her, but Stella waved my words away. "I wish some of this career success had spilled over to my private life," she sighed, "but I guess my infertility problems are my own fault, I just didn't get it together early enough."

Stella filled me in on her early history.

I was engaged to this guy in graduate school, but he slept with a friend of mine so we broke up. Then, after getting my degree—Ph.D.s take forever at Duke—I started teaching and found myself dealing with a difficult job market and a nomadic life: a year at the University of California at Santa Cruz filling in for someone on leave, three years at Chapel Hill, a year at Brandeis, and finally a tenure-track position at Vanderbilt. With all this moving around I didn't meet someone I could be serious about until I got to Vanderbilt. By then I was 37 and didn't waste any time. John and I met, married, and started trying to have a baby all within a year. But the baby-making bit wasn't easy for us. I didn't get pregnant the first six months, or the next, or the next.

For me this was a big deal. I'm the kind of person who has always wanted children—I've wanted to be a mom all my life. So I was deeply shocked by the idea I might be infertile. How could this be happening to me? I had worked so hard to stay in great physical shape. One thing was clear—I wanted to start the fertility workups straightaway so as to not lose any time. But I ran into an unexpected problem—a husband who was dragging his feet.

For months we talked past each other. He carried on about the expense of the procedures and how we might just luck out if we waited. And I carried on about my dwindling egg supply and how we needed to act now. Although I was only 38 I could actually feel myself becoming less fertile. My periods were getting lighter, and my breasts no longer felt as heavy or as tender when I ovulated. My body seemed to be telling me that I was coming to the end of the time when I could become pregnant.

Don't get me wrong, John's a kind man and in the end he did the right thing and tried to support me. But our instincts were at odds. Deep down I knew that I had only this narrow window—that my time was running out—while deep down he knew that he could have children for years to come. It's not at all that he doesn't want kids. He wants them, but in a nonurgent, abstract kind of way.

I don't see my husband's eyes being drawn to other people's children while mine are drawn like magnets. I lean over and smile at infants in baby carriages and marvel at the sensations in my body. It's as though my flesh yearns to hold and hug a small body. I sit and watch toddlers in playgrounds and listen for their laughter. The magic of a small child's laugh—those cascading peals of pure joy—I always shiver at the beauty of it.

Well, we finally sought help, and after four months on Clomid I got pregnant. We were ecstatic for eleven all-too-short weeks. Then I miscarried. It was called a "missed miscarriage," which meant that there was no traumatic event, the baby just died in utero. I went for a sonogram and the doctor couldn't find a heartbeat. I will never forget the agony of seeing our partially formed baby outlined on the screen—stiff, still and lifeless. That first loss was hard, very hard.

A few months later we tried again. This time I took Clomid and did something called HSG—a procedure that involves shooting stuff into your fallopian tubes to make sure that they are super clear. And sure enough I got pregnant. This time I miscarried in week thirteen. Again, it was a "missed miscarriage." This second loss was even harder. We had made it to the three-month mark and were beginning to believe we would have this baby. We had even picked out some names.

After the second miscarriage we got deadly serious. We took out a second mortgage on our house and signed up for IVF. Twelve months and three cycles later I got pregnant again, only to miscarry in week five. This pregnancy was over in a blink of an eye. At the time I told myself that this loss wasn't as bad as the others because it was so early. Whether or not this was true, I knew I needed to build some kind of wall between me and my colossal, cumulative grief.

Those IVF cycles were completely debilitating—and I'm not just talking about the money. For months we were whiplashed by a treatment regime that jerked us from hope to despair. The drugs and the procedures created huge stresses in my marriage and even undermined the way I felt about my body. I began to resent my sexual organs. I mean, if these parts and these functions turn out to be completely useless, how can I do anything but resent my big breasts and bloody periods. They are merely burdensome.

So after the third miscarriage we had to walk away—to heal our wounds and recoup our various losses. That was two and a half years ago. This

conference is my first stab at reacquainting myself
with whatever options are left. You know the
advice handed out to our generation was very
problematic. We were told: "Do what men do.
Work your tail off until you're established in your
field. Sacrifice what you need to for your career."
But now I think, if you want children "cloning the
male, competitive model" doesn't work.

I'm forever telling my women students: Don't
be afraid of letting go of a half-built career. We are
smart, well-educated, and life is long. Career
opportunities can be recaptured. Don't waste that
small window of fertility. Don't live to regret not
having had a child.[7]

As is clear from these stories, some of the most heartfelt
struggles of the breakthrough generation have centered on the attempt to snatch a child from the jaws of
menopause. A few succeed; most do not. Unlimited
resources and a great deal of good luck help explain
why Wendy Wasserstein was successful and Stella
Parsons was not. Some of the women who fail to get
pregnant subsequently go on to adopt a child—often on
their own.

Mary Farrell, 46, and I had dinner a week before she
went to China to pick up her infant daughter. It was a

27-hour trip to Guilin and Mary was taking her father with her to help with the logistical challenges. I found it achingly poignant that her frail father—a 75-year-old man with severe arthritis—was the only person in her life willing and able to help her collect her new baby.

Mary was a fellow activist in Labour Party politics. We had gotten to know one another in 1991 when I spent several months in the United Kingdom. At that point in her career she was running a high-profile child advocacy organization. In the mid-1990s she went back to get an MBA from the London Business School, and she is now a partner in a small management consulting firm based in Cambridge. Mary had turned 45 a year earlier, a birthday that triggered a great deal of soul searching. A few months after that she bought a house—complete with garden and swing set—and started down the road to adoption. Over dinner Mary showed me pictures of seven-month-old Kerry—an impossibly cute Chinese baby. Mary glowed and sparkled as she talked of finally meeting her small daughter.

"I can't wait to hug and hold her. In fact, I plan on not letting go of her for weeks to make up to her for having spent the first months of life in an orphanage. I'm convinced that if we are inseparable for three months—if she sleeps with me and if I just carry her around in a Snugli during the day—we can jump-start the whole bonding process. I'm determined to make this baby girl feel cherished."

Mary explained that turning 45 on her own—no husband, no children—had been excruciating. But painful as this birthday was, it had forced her to admit that she was now unlikely to get married. "And yet I couldn't give up on motherhood. To me it is the ultimate act of participation in the future—of hopefulness in the future. I think that the radical out-of-controlness of it will be good for me—will open me up in ways I cannot yet know. I have so fine-tuned and planned my life.

"I wish I had done it before. But it's only recently that I've had a measure of financial security. Even now I feel it's pretty risky. Most of our clients are in e-commerce and at least some of them have gone belly up over this last year. Several of my friends advised me to wait until the economy stabilizes again. But I am already old to be a first-time mom. I can't keep on putting off the important things in life. On my deathbed, a rough patch in my career won't seem nearly as important as having raised a daughter."

Later on in the evening Mary talked thoughtfully about her mother and father. "You know, my parents have been like rocks in this whole process. I found them pretty rigid growing up—being strict Catholics they had too many rules—but they have this extraordinary veneration for children and have tried so hard to support me in my efforts to adopt. I suppose it would have been harder for them had I gotten pregnant as a single woman. The whole issue of fatherhood is hugely important to them. They would have hated the notion of using a man—through deceit or through contract—for his sperm and then to disconnect him from his children. I must say that I agree with them."[8]

Of course, it's no longer unusual for a professional woman to adopt a child on her own, but that doesn't make single-motherhood any easier. Patricia Williams, 48, is a legal scholar, political activist, and professor at Columbia Law School. For years she had promised herself if she weren't married by forty she would just go ahead and adopt a baby.

"So, a few days after the big birthday I called an agency. They said no problem, they had babies—one of the few advantages of being an African-American woman is that if you want to adopt there are all kinds of unwanted children out there. Six months later I adopted my son. It was love at first sight. He was irresistible. My dominant emotion was that of gratitude. I mean, it's such an extraordinary privilege to be needed so much—to matter so powerfully to another human being. He has transformed my priorities more deeply than I thought possible. Every now and then I try to think through what my life would have been like if I had not adopted, but I can't do it, the hole is just too big."

Williams graduated from Wellesley College in 1971 and Harvard Law School in 1975, one of nine black women in a graduating class of 500. In her words, "the civil rights struggle got me to Wellesley, but going to law school was absolutely a gift of the women's movement. I had no ambition prior to college, but my ambition grew as the opportunities for people like me grew. I started off studying very traditional subjects (French and art history), but in my sophomore year they started a program that allowed Wellesley students to take courses at MIT. Suddenly my world expanded. I ended up majoring in urban studies with the idea of going to Harvard Law School, becoming an activist lawyer and changing the world. It was as simple as that.

"After law school I went to work as a prosecutor for the city of Los Angeles in the Department of Consumer Protection—it was the first time a woman of color had held such a position. I then went to work for the Legal Aid Corporation. In 1980 I joined the faculty at UCLA, and after a stint at Wisconsin came to Columbia in the early 1990s. For the last twenty years I have been a teacher, a writer, and an activist—mostly around issues of race and gender."

Talking about professional things is easy for Williams. She describes her work life as "a fairly smooth arc." Not that it was in any way easy or automatic. As she points out, her career was critically dependent on the success of the civil rights and feminist struggles. But once the new opportunities were in place, an ambitious career became something she could grapple with and struggle for. In the end she was able to build an enviable professional life, one which carried with it conventional attributes of success— status and earning power—and was also deeply meaningful to her.

Private life has been much more problematic for Williams. The only relationship that came close to marriage involved a man she dated while at Wellesley and during her first year at Harvard Law—now some 25 years ago. In her view, "It broke up because he saw me as too competitive. He was only fine with my going to law school if I was willing to go to work for his career—to be his support team. Once it became clear that I had independent ambitions, he broke things off. Most of the guys at Harvard Law were a lot more comfortable dating undergraduates at Wellesley and BU than classmates at the law school. I guess we were just too threatening.

"After law school social life just drained away. My various career moves haven't helped. Madison—a bedroom community dominated by married couples—was particularly bleak for a single, black, female professional. To be honest, at 48 I've pretty much given up."

Williams has a thoughtful perspective on single-parenthood. "Raising a child as a single person has been a wonderful experience, but it has also been terrifying. My son is a big person, already taller and heavier than I am. He weighs 111 pounds and is only seven years old. I worry so much when I see him walking down city streets. I pepper him with advice—don't walk in the shadows, don't put your hands in your pockets. But I still ache with worry. To a racist cop he already looks large and menacing—anything could happen.

"It's intensely lonely—being on my own and raising a child. There's no one to share the good times with—or the bad times. There are so many hours when I crave adult companionship. No one should underestimate the toll."[9]

A powerful drumbeat echoes through the stories of Wendy, Stella, Mary, and Patricia: The challenges of late-in-life motherhood are extraordinarily real. Whether you go the IVF route or the adoption route the deterrents are huge, the hurdles high. If you are a forty-something woman yearning for motherhood, you'd better be prepared to pay an extremely high price for a child—financially and emotionally.

Of course many women do not even get as far as trying to birth—or adopt—that premenopausal baby. I talked to a whole cluster of women who became derailed at an earlier stage by high-maintenance careers and skittish partners. For them, the pivotal struggles did not center on children, rather, they centered on finding the right man while there was still time to allow for the possibility of having children—or at least a child. Male attitudes are critical here. As Wendy points out in *The Heidi Chronicles,* a man is often reluctant to choose an A+ woman because an A+ woman might mean serious competition. It must be ten years since I saw this play, but I still remember that famous scene in which Scoop Rosenbaum explains to Heidi why he decided to marry Lisa instead of her. Scoop's words sent shivers down my spine because I realized how fortunate I was to have found a man capable of both loving and living with an accomplished woman.

> SCOOP: Let's say we married and I asked you to
> devote the, say, next ten years of your life to me.
> To making me a home and a family so secure that
> I could with some confidence go out into the
> world each day and attempt to make an A . . .

You'd say, "Why can't we be partners? Why can't
we both go out into the world and get an A?" And
you'd be absolutely valid and correct . . .

HEIDI: But Lisa . . .

SCOOP: Do I love her, as your friend asked me?
She's the best I can do. Is she an A+? A- maybe,
but not an A+ . . . I couldn't dangle you anymore,
and that's why I got married today . . . You want
other things in life than I do.

HEIDI: Really? Like what?

SCOOP: Self-fulfillment. Self-determination. Self-
exaggeration.

HEIDI: That's exactly what you want.

SCOOP: Right. Then you'd be competing with
me.[10]

Tamara Adler, 43, managing director of Deutsche Bank
in London, knows this territory all too well. In
December 2000, we were introduced by a close, mutual
friend and on one of my trips to the United Kingdom she
invited me to join her for an early breakfast in her office.
In the depths of winter London is not an early-morning
city, and as I walked along an almost-deserted Great
Winchester Street at 7:30 A.M. just as dawn was breaking, I wondered if I had gotten the time and place right.

But a slim, elegant, smiling woman was waiting for me at the elevator bank on the second floor of the Deutsche Bank building, and over strong tea and digestive biscuits we talked—and talked—and talked. A few well-placed questions opened a floodgate. This subject matter was clearly on her mind.

Adler would dearly love to have a husband and children and has given much thought to why family hasn't happened for her. She talks about the obvious practical challenges. "I can't imagine how I could raise a family in the job I have now. Travel is a real killer. I'm gone about two and a half days a week. For instance, I'm going to South Africa tomorrow and won't be back until Sunday. And then there's business entertaining—when I'm in town I'm involved in about three dinners a week."

But logistical challenges are not uppermost in her mind. She now has a measure of market power and could find a different kind of job—one, for example, that does not require travel. Much more difficult than dealing with the logistics is finding a successful man who would comfortably tolerate her level of success. Adler is totally uninterested in having a child on her own—she feels that it would be much too difficult and unfair to the child—so this issue of finding a man is absolutely critical if she is going to have a baby before it's too late.

Adler talked eloquently about how ambitious

careers discriminated against women. She didn't
mean in the usual sense—opportunities are, after all,
wide open these days—but in the sense that it is much
easier for men to find the right kind of emotional and
practical support than it is for their female colleagues.

In her words, "In the rarefied upper reaches of high-
altitude careers, where the air is thin and it's hard to
breathe, men have a much easier time finding oxygen."

They find oxygen in the form of women who will
coddle their egos and make them feel like a king
or some other kind of superior being.

What any hard-driving, high-performing individual wants at the end of a fourteen-hour day is
a partner who says, "Wow, you're amazing." Or
"Wow, what a killing you made today, you must
be exhausted—let me rub your back/get you a
drink/cook your dinner." High-earning successful
men have access to a large pool of women—many
of them young, beautiful, and sexy—who are
ready to provide oxygen at a drop of a hat. It's
from this pool that they select a mate.

The hard fact is that most successful men are
not interested in acquiring a peer as a partner.
Another high-altitude mountaineer might be enormously stimulating, but can she be relied on to
pony up oxygen on a regular basis? Probably not.
Familiarity really does breed contempt. It's hard
to say, "Wow!" and look adoring if you are in the

throes of a similar career struggle. You are much
more likely to see the warts and the glitches.
Besides which, you have your own urgent need for
oxygen, and yearn to be pampered and coddled in
your own right.

As Adler points out, the "wow" factor is particularly
powerful in the early years of a career, which is precisely when most ambitious men get married. "Late
twenties, early thirties, this is when all of us professionals are still wobbly—we have these spindly horse
legs and can easily be pushed over. At this stage in life,
sex and admiration go a long way to smoothing out the
rough edges."

Tamara Adler grew up in Florida, Connecticut, and
Washington, D.C. She attended Wellesley and then
went on to graduate from Northwestern Law School in
1982. Her career was on the fast track from the word
go. She started off as an associate in the New York law
firm Simpson, Thacher and Bartlett, but quickly
became bored with corporate law. As she put it, "mark-
ing up the same legal document for the eighty-fifth
time soon lost its appeal." So she moved to Goldman
Sachs and became part of an intense, deal-driven, work
environment. Adler put in fourteen-hour days, worked
every Sunday, and traveled 30 percent of the time.
After a brief interlude in Washington, Adler came to
London—to head up the European Securitization

Group at Deutsche Bank. As the most senior woman at Deutsche Bank, she was recently voted one of the ten most powerful women in the city of London.

Looking into the future, Adler has an interesting perspective on her options. "Over the last couple of years I've begun to date older, divorced guys. Men who have done the success thing and the family thing and are now looking for companionship. I fit in with their needs because they now want real conversations with someone who is a player in their world. And they fit in with my needs because these older men are grown-up enough—mellow enough—to give a little oxygen."

Adler leaned forward and her eyes sparkled. "I can't tell you what it feels like to be newly in demand," she said. "All of a sudden it's a different ball game." She paused. "But I don't kid myself. Even if I end up marrying one of these older men—and I think I may—I won't be able to have children. None of these guys is remotely interested in having another set of children. And that makes me enormously sad. I mean, what will I think about that when I'm sixty-five? Will I regret not having had children? Of course I will."[11]

Charlene Martin[12], 44, small business owner and sometime lawyer, is also disarmingly direct: "This juggling act, trying to have a serious relationship as well as a

career, is hard for any ambitious woman, but I tell
you, it's well nigh impossible for an ambitious, black
woman. We just face different odds."

A friend of a close friend, Martin grew up on the
wrong side of the tracks in San Antonio, Texas. By her
own account, even as a child she was about "the most
driven individual you could ever hope to meet."
Dogged determination and hard work paid off. By
1976 Martin was a freshman at Harvard College and
by 1985 she was a newly minted lawyer working as an
associate in a prestigious Texas law firm. The only
problem was, she hated it. In her words,

> The Texas culture and the cowboy mentality
> didn't help, but it was more than that. In concrete
> ways, women were still second-class citizens
> at this firm. We were not allowed to deal with
> corporate transactions; the perception was we
> couldn't deal with the big boys in the conference
> room. We were called "lady lawyers" and were
> shuttled off to trusts and estates where we
> couldn't do much harm. When I joined this firm,
> out of approximately 120 partners, three were
> women. I was only there a year. I remember so
> clearly the conversation that triggered my
> resignation—it's as though it happened yesterday.
>
> One of the senior partners came into my office
> to talk about a case I was working on about
> property rights and oil. He said, "Oh yeah, those

properties belong to R. Cummings. You know how Cummings made money? He figured out a way to get niggers to give their oil holdings to the oil companies . . . back in the old days, the niggers would get the worst land, the rockiest land that didn't produce much, but it turned out that the rockiest land had oil on it. So Cummings worked out a way to get that land for a couple of bucks. He was real persuasive."

Well, I was deeply offended by this conversation and told a colleague about it and soon I had a whole committee of people coming into my office explaining that this senior partner didn't mean any harm, he was just using a word his daddy had used. Someone even tried to convince me that for someone from the old school, "nigger" was a term of affection!

Despite the protestations, I resigned and started looking for a job in the Northeast. I decided it was hard enough being a "lady lawyer"—why compound my problems by working in a blatantly racist city? So I came to New York and went to work for a big firm.

From the first week on the job I clinked into super-driven mode, got very focused, and planned on making partner. It's hard to grasp how hard I worked. I mean, I worked all the time—an easy thirteen hours a day, six days a week, and at least some hours on Sunday. I ate so much Chinese take-out that when I left private practice I vowed I would never eat Chinese food again.

I measured the effect of these brutal hours on my social life by how many beeps there were on my message machine when I got home at night. Two years into this job there were no beeps because everyone knew that either I wasn't there, or if I was there, I couldn't go anywhere or make any plans. Dinner dates had to be after 10:00 P.M. and weekend trips were out of the question.

I'll never forget the elation at being released at 5:30 P.M. one Saturday evening and being told I didn't have to work anymore that weekend. I thought, God, what an embarrassment of riches. I have this wonderful long weekend! I had become so accustomed to working until 10:00 P.M. on Saturday and putting in another six hours on Sunday that I really felt I had been given a vacation.

I was routinely tortured by a certain partner— he wasn't particularly vicious, he just reflected the culture of the firm. He used to bounce into my office at 9:30 P.M. and say, "Okay, I have a project for you. It's gotta get done. I don't care how you do it, but when I come in at 9:30 A.M. tomorrow morning, I want it finished and on my desk." So there were lots of nights when I didn't go home until three in the morning, and others when I didn't go home at all. On average I had an all-nighter every three weeks or so.

The crazy thing is that all this effort was for naught. After selling my soul for three years I was fired. The stock market took a nosedive and they eliminated thirty positions, including mine. For me, this was a wake-up call. There I was, twenty-nine years old and I could hardly remember anything that had happened to me in three years. I had worked so hard that this whole period was a blur. So I decided to get a life. I left private practice and went to work for a Japanese company, a company where, I was told, in-house lawyers put in a ten-hour day and never worked weekends. I thought this new job might give me a chance to have a relationship, to meet some man I might marry and have children with.

At the beginning, things looked as though they might pan out. I met this beautiful African-American guy—a divorcé with two lovely daughters. He was in agony about not seeing his children enough and needed all kinds of support. I was deeply in love and tried to come through for him. I mean, I really thought he was the man for me. But just about the time he started putting out feelers and asking how I felt about getting married, the company told me I needed to spend time in Japan. I was doing well at the company and if I was to progress further I needed to spend some years at the head office. Now I wasn't at all clear that I would take this posting, but this man was so threatened by the fact I was even entertaining the possibility of moving to Japan that he broke up with me. I was devastated.

Martin ultimately did move to Japan, where the general counsel took her under his wing and she started to get promoted. Over the next few years, work life got much more hectic and her ten-hour day turned into a thirteen-hour day, once again crowding out her personal life. Martin tries to be fair-minded: "Don't get me wrong, the company treated me well and during the ten years I spent with them. I built up a significant measure of financial independence, but there was no way I could stay with the company and develop a rich, private life. So three years ago I bailed out. I quit my job, took my savings, and opened a restaurant in Tribeca. It's been incredibly exhilarating—taking my hard-won financial freedom and using it to tap into my creativity. I've always loved painting and photography, and it's an enormous privilege to make these things the stuff of everyday life." Looking back at her decision-making over the last twenty years, Martin has mixed feelings.

"I fault myself for barreling forward and not paying

enough attention to the quality of my life. I should have reinvented my professional life earlier than I did. That way, I might have been able to have a family." Martin paused, and then said with evident pain: "My big regret is not having had children. When my youngest sister had a child a few years ago—the first grandchild in my family—great waves of longing swept over me. It was incredibly difficult."

This regret is all mixed up with not having found a man because for Martin, "marriage and children is a package. I have no romantic notions about the joys of being a single mother. My mother raised three children on her own. I've seen it up close and it's brutally hard. Now, like a lot of women I did go through a period of saying, 'If I turn forty and I don't have a relationship, I will think about adopting.' But then I conceived the idea of the restaurant and got into this debate with myself about which was more important to me— having a child or having the restaurant. And I chose a restaurant." She paused and then said quietly and thoughtfully, "But this is not a choice I wanted to deal with. If there had been a man in my life it would have been a no-brainer, I would have done both.

"At this point I've pretty much given up on men. I mean, it's just too competitive. A few months ago a guy friend of mine separated from his wife and within hours women were hitting on him—giving him their phone numbers, buying theater tickets, inviting him out to dinner. The fact is there are about five of us to one of them. Black, professional, unattached men are as rare as hen's teeth. And they know it. Some of them feel entitled to an extraordinary amount of attention. They don't even try to disguise it. One man told me straight out it was admiration he wanted from a woman. But I think he meant adoration."[13]

Sue Palmer, 49, International Marketing Communications Director of Grant Thornton, the London-based accounting firm, has also given up on men. "Ten years ago an extremely valued personal assistant of mine told me at the end of a particularly grueling seventy-hour week, 'You know, Sue, you couldn't have a torrid love affair if you wanted to.' And I shot right back: 'I couldn't have a *tepid* love affair if I wanted to.' That exchange sums up the situation. For twenty-five years this career of mine has sat in the center of my life, using up prime time. As a result, relationships and the possibility of marriage and children were just crowded out. I mean I never decided that I didn't want a family, in fact I would love to have had a family. That phrase, 'a creeping nonchoice,' pretty much sums up what happened to me."

Palmer found climbing the first rungs of the career ladder extremely difficult. As a milkman's daughter from North Yorkshire, she had more than the usual number of hurdles to clear. From the local, state secondary school she won admission to Cambridge (we were at the same college a few years apart) and, upon graduation, joined Marks and Spencer as a graduate trainee, one of a small handful of women to join the program that year. A few years later she went back to business school to get an MBA. She then joined Grant Thornton, and over the years rose through the ranks to become the only woman on the management committee of this global accounting firm. According to Palmer,

There are no secrets to success in the business world. Able individuals merely have to put together the determination and grit to perform at a very high level. If this involves extraordinarily long hours and a brutal travel schedule, so be it.

About ten years ago, round about the time I realized I would most probably not get married and not have kids, I met this industrial psychologist. I actually remember the circumstances. We were at some conference and he and I went for a long walk along a river. He was a good listener and I opened up telling him of the disappointments I was wrestling with, and he told me that to remain strong and vital I needed to find something in life that could be as important to me as children. If I could do this—find some interest that had deep, personal meaning—it would force me to balance my life. Otherwise, there was a danger my soul would shrivel—I still remember his exact words—and I could become some kind of unidimensional workaholic.

This conversation had such a profound impact. I mean, I just knew he was right. For several years I had tried to force myself to take some time off— to relax, to wind down. But I'm a driven person and it's awfully hard to curtail work—to do nothing in particular. So the idea of deliberately finding a counterpoint in my life seemed brilliant.

A little while later I became deeply involved in efforts to support a struggling orchestra in North London. And just this last year I was invited to become a trustee of the Heritage Lottery Fund— now a 300-million-pounds-a-year operation. This volunteer position brings with it a tremendous potential to do good since I get to decide the merits of projects that run the gamut from wetlands to puppets. These are now my babies and I know they are food for my soul.

I had dinner with Sue Palmer just before Christmas 2000, and she was arranging for a car to bring her elderly parents—now deep in their eighties—from Yorkshire to her home in London for the holidays. As she fussed over the arrangements for this frail pair—how big a car, how many stops it should make—she was reminded not only of their dependence on her, but of her dependence on them. "They always come to me for Christmas. I love having them. In fact, I'm not sure what I will do at Christmas when they are gone." She paused, and then added reflectively, "You know, whenever you think you've come to terms with it—this business of not having children—it crops up again in another form. I try not to think about it, but when my parents die, I'll have to deal with not having kids yet again. I now see it as a rolling loss.[14]

Charlene Martin and Sue Palmer share much more than their sadness at not having had children. These immensely able women had the courage and good sense to take the passion and compassion they might have invested in children, and channel it into something else—something thoroughly worthwhile. I find this deeply inspiring. Childlessness need not shrivel the soul or shrink the spirit. These generous-spirited women—and others I interviewed for this book—had the guts to turn their creative energies elsewhere, to projects and endeavors that will have lasting benefit to themselves and others.

When I first met Holly Atkinson, 47, some three years ago, I remember thinking that if anyone were to ask me which woman seemed destined to have it all, it would be this woman. Atkinson has the blond page boy and finely wrought profile of a classic American beauty—a veritable Grace Kelly look-alike. She also happens to be a physician with a high-powered, high-earning job in the e-commerce sector.

As a young woman, Atkinson spent a great deal of time and energy breaking the mold of what was expected of women. A member of the class of 1974 at Colgate University (the first class to admit women), she went on to attend the University of Rochester School of Medicine where she was one of seven women in a graduating class of 103. She remembers medical school as a pretty dreadful experience.

> Sexual harassment was flagrant. I mean, things were done to us routinely that are against the law these days. In our anatomy class the professor would "accidentally on purpose" slip in some pornographic slides just to embarrass the women. The guys thought it was a great joke. Crude pranks and sexually explicit notes were standard fare.
>
> My reaction was to hunker down and perform. I didn't particularly bond with other women or they with me. I guess we were too isolated and too scared. The only time sisterhood was important was when we messed up—then it reflected on our gender.
>
> I remember one time a surgeon gave me the

opportunity to stitch someone up in the operating room. Now, I was very good at this. My mother had taught me how to embroider vestments for the church. From the time I was seven we used to sit together and embroider these gorgeous brocades. She had high standards. We would wear white gloves and use silk thread of the finest quality that we ordered from England. By the time I was a teenager I was a great seamstress.

So I set to work sewing up this person, who happened to be rather obese. Closing up an obese person is tricky. The skin doesn't fit back together neatly, so it's like putting up a hem on a flared skirt. But I figured out a stitch that solved the problem, and there I was just whipping along. I get to the end of the closure and it is near perfect—no ripples or pouches, no extra skin hanging out. Then this arrogant son of a bitch surgeon looks at me and says, "Well I'll be darned, a woman who can sew." Then he points to my handiwork and starts to chortle. And his sidekicks—the male residents—join in.

Something snapped. I mean I was enraged. This awful man had no idea of how proud I was of my sewing skills, of how deep it went for me. I wanted to throttle him—or at the very least stick him with my needle. But in the end all I did was turn away—in more senses than one. It was the conceit and condescension of men like him that

made me decide not to become a surgeon. And
that's a real pity. I'm fabulous with my hands.

Despite these early struggles, the arc of Atkinson's
career has been smooth and strong. After medical
school she decided to go into medical journalism. She
spent two years with the *Walter Cronkite Show,* a science and medical news program, and then became the
on-air medical correspondent for the *CBS Morning
News.* This was followed by senior positions at
Lifetime and Reuters (where she built Reuters Health,
a daily news service for physicians). In 1998 she was
named CEO of HealthAnswers.com. By her own
admission her personal life has been a lot less linear—
and, at least until recently, a lot less successful.

In 1983 she married a man 17 years older than she
was.

Grant was this computer guru at IBM. I think I
was drawn to him because he was kind, consider-
ate, courteous, and not at all threatened by me. He
was already pretty established. He had this big
career, an ex-wife, and three grown children.
A couple of years into the marriage it became
clear that I really wanted children and Grant did
his best to make that possible by going through a
procedure to reverse a vasectomy he had gotten
toward the end of his first marriage. When we
failed to get pregnant we went through an infertil-

ity workup and discovered that I had all kinds of scar tissue from injuries I sustained when I ruptured my appendix some years back. We were told that IVF was our only shot at having a child. But by this time there was a lot of conflict in the marriage and we were running out of steam.

It's hard to talk about . . . there was a lot of anguish. A couple of years later we got divorced. I was forty. I tell you forty is a terrible age to get divorced. The fact that I was childless and alone hit me like a ton of bricks.

For years I had known that the clock was ticking, but I kept thinking, it's ticking, but not for me. Because I'm powerful, because I've worked hard and done well. Besides which, I'm a doctor and all doctors indulge in magical thinking. Some of the worst smokers are oncologists. They think that somehow their profession is going to protect them from the ravages of cancer. Not true. But I'm guilty of the same kind of magical thinking. Yeah, the clock is ticking and the odds are going down, but for some reason I will always have a choice. And then I hit forty. No husband, no kid. Not now, not ever. I cried myself to sleep for weeks.

She paused. Her voice had become low and seemed thinned out by pain.

You know people look at someone like me—
someone who's attractive, successful, and doesn't
have kids—and think, oh she doesn't like kids. Or,
she gave up kids for her career. Sometimes people
even say these things to my face. And it makes me
see red because I'm so clear on this: *I didn't make
a choice not to have kids.*

A couple of years ago I started thinking about
adopting a Chinese girl on my own. More recently
I asked my sister if she would give me some of her
eggs. I guess I didn't think I would meet the right
man. Or at least I wasn't holding my breath. I'd
worked it out in my mind that at my age there
were three types of men.

First there are the good guys, and they're
taken. These are the ones who can make a commitment. A second type is a man who has not been
married and either he is gay, or he is so screwed up
you don't want him. Then there is a third
category, and these guys may be the worst of all.
They are married but in huge turmoil. They've
fallen out of love with their wife and are trying to
figure out whether to get divorced or not.

And then Holly Atkinson smiled—the first smile in
our two-hour conversation. "I was such a cynic, but
happily I was so wrong. Last year I met this wonderful
man and we have fallen in love. We are about to
announce our engagement. Can you believe that?" And

this beautiful woman broke into peals of laughter. She looked about as radiant as it's possible to be.

Before we parted that day, Atkinson had one last pensive thought about children. "You know, I would love nothing more than to have a child with Galen . . . and I never will. I'm just too old. Now we could adopt or we could do donor eggs, but we will never have a child that is ours—that is, his and mine. It's an unspeakable loss not to be able to have that.[15]

Before closing this first chapter I want to share the life story of a woman who has successfully balanced her life. Clearly there are women in the breakthrough generation who managed to achieve both a high-flying career and a family. Molly Friedrich, 49, literary agent, wife, and mother of three is a case in point.

> When I graduated from Barnard in '74 I was seethingly ambitious. Looking back I must have been quite frightening. Not that I knew what I wanted to do. But I knew this much: that I needed to plunge in and work as hard as I knew how during my twenties. But I also knew I wanted to get married and have children, and that I needed to factor this in early on. I couldn't imagine building a life without children in it.
>
> I started work at Doubleday, first as an intern, then as a secretary in the trade division. After two

years I got this extraordinary promotion. I was invited to run Anchor Press publicity—a huge job for a twenty-four-year-old. There I was, the proud possessor of a midtown office, a secretary, an expense account, and the heady responsibility of promoting 133 books a year.

I discovered that I was really good at my new job. I guess I'm a natural born salesperson—I could literally sell ice cream to Eskimos. It was soon clear to me that I could build myself a hugely successful career in corporate publishing. The sky was the limit. Yet two years later I was out of there.

I had just gotten married—to someone I had met at college—and Mark and I were trying to figure out how to start a family. I looked around the publishing world and saw that very few of the senior women had children. The handful of mothers I knew were underpaid, overworked, and seemed to have a telephone relationship with their children. This is not what I wanted. So I decided to seek out something more entrepreneurial and flexible—becoming a literary agent appeared to fit the bill. The successful agents I knew called the shots and had a great deal of control.

I put out the word and a literary agent who operated out of her home on the Upper East Side offered me a job as her assistant. I accepted with alacrity, although at the time all my friends thought I had lost my mind. I mean, here I was taking a one-third cut in salary, and leaving a glamorous job with a secretary to go be someone else's secretary. The reality of this new job was a little worse than I let on, because my duties included picking up steaming mounds of dog shit when I arrived for work in the morning.

But it all worked out. I learned the business and a year later I moved on to the Aaron Priest Agency, where I have been ever since. It was a lateral move—again, as an assistant—but over time I developed a client list of my own and went onto a commission basis. I've worked extremely hard to attract and retain my wonderful authors, but I've also had some lucky breaks. For example, Frank McCourt and Melissa Bank literally fell into my lap. This was blind luck.

The thing I'm most proud of is that I have taken advantage of my entrepreneurial job to carve out a great deal of time for my family. When our first child was born in '81 I started leaving the office at 4:00 P.M. When our second child was born in '86 I stopped going into the office on Friday. And when we adopted a third child in '97 Monday went by the board. It's one up for Aaron that he has always been confident I could produce with this increasingly minimal schedule.

To be honest, my part-time work life is a long

way from being easy or obvious. Success tends to beget success and I am inundated with requests to represent authors. I must get 200 letters a week from authors wanting me to take them on. But since I don't want work to invade any more of my life, I nearly always say no. Very occasionally someone comes along who is tremendously exciting and then I capitulate and say yes, but mostly I hold these pressures at bay. I have developed some pretty effective strategies. For example, I don't do e-mail, I don't use a cell phone, and I remain inaccessible to my authors on weekends. But the main part of my strategy is sticking to a three-day workweek and allowing myself the space to enjoy my family. Bouncing on the trampoline with my four-year-old, getting to know my fifteen-year-old's boyfriend, sharing the foreign-language enthusiasms of my twenty-year-old. These are some of the things I have created time to savor.

I love my life. It is a glorious privilege to have both a personal and a professional life that are deeply satisfying. I probably would not make a good full-time mother—I am way too intense. This balance is good for me.

But I do understand that every week of my life is a high-wire act and it's not for the fainthearted. One thing that gets squeezed out is time for me. I dream about going to a museum all by myself and not feeling guilty. Or just taking a half day and getting a pedicure. These are impossible luxuries.

One piece of advice for young women. Do a whole lot of planning early on. Be as strategic about your personal life as you are about your career. And find an occupation where you can bend the rules. Then, work hard enough to deserve having those rules bent for you.[16]

These, then, are some representatives of the break-through generation: nine enormously accomplished and courageous women who have elected to talk openly about their lives and their struggles. The generosity of spirit and raw, unflinching honesty that imbue these voices is palpable—and hugely impressive. How often do successful people with images to hone and reputations to protect make themselves vulnerable in order to help others? Almost never. These stories, therefore, constitute a rare and precious gift from one generation to the next, and I, for one, am both touched and grateful.

When I asked these women why they were willing to open up their lives—exposing wounds, reliving pain—several told me straight out that they feared that conditions and choices had not changed and they wanted to forewarn and forearm younger women. Stella Parsons put it well. "Young women deserve to be told the unvarnished truth," she said. "It will help them deal with reality." At bottom, these big-hearted, gutsy women feel the unfairness of a society that continues to thrust cruel choices on women. They want their younger sisters to have a better shot at getting what they want out of life. "After all," said Mary Farrell, "don't most men—no matter how high-achieving—routinely count on having both a career and a family?

A final note. In *An American Daughter*—the darkest of Wendy Wasserstein's plays—the female lead, Lyssa Dent, confronts head-on the special challenges women face when they attempt to have it all. At the beginning of the play, Lyssa appears to have achieved across-the-board success. She has a prominent career, an established marriage, and two well-adjusted children. Yet, as the play progresses she is shot down in a "jury-gate" scandal and loses the chance of being named surgeon general of the United States. As the president, the press, various friends—and even her husband—gang up on her, Lyssa takes time to reflect, with edge and bitterness, on the universal resentment provoked by successful women. "There's a perception out there that some women just have too much," she tells her loyal friend Judith Kaufman.[17]

Lyssa draws attention to an exceedingly important point. If young women are to improve their options and widen their choices, they will need to get over this first hurdle: how to combat the attitude so prevalent in our culture that it is somehow unseemly—or greedy—for a woman to want success in more than one sphere of life. Somehow a perception has emerged that a woman isn't a woman unless her life is riddled with sacrifice. Remember how Hillary Clinton's approval ratings tanked when she was running the healthcare initiative and soared when she was publicly humiliated by her husband's philanderings?

I can't tell you how many times women I interviewed apologized for "wanting it all." It always made me angry. I mean, it isn't as though these women were standing in line for handouts. They were quite prepared to shoulder more than their fair share of the work involved in having both career and family. So why on earth shouldn't they feel entitled to rich, multidimensional lives? At the end of the day, women simply want the choices in love and work that men take so completely for granted.

2

THE SOBERING FACTS

*I*N JANUARY 2001, IN PARTNERSHIP with Harris Interactive and the National Parenting Association, I fielded a nationwide survey designed to explore the professional and private lives of highly educated/high-earning women. In this survey, called *High-Achieving Women, 2001,* we targeted the top 10 percent of women—measured in terms of earning power—and focused on two age groups: the breakthrough generation, ages 41–55, and their younger peers, 28–40. We distinguished between high-achievers (those earning over $55,000 or $65,000 depending on age) and ultra-achievers (those earning over $100,000), and included a sample of "high-potential" women—

highly qualified women who have left their careers, mainly for family reasons. In addition, we added in a small sample of men.[1]

The findings of this survey are startling—and sobering. Here are some of the highlights:

CHILDLESSNESS HAUNTS THE EXECUTIVE SUITE

Thirty-three percent of high-achieving women are childless at age 40, and this figure rises to 42 percent in corporate America.[2] Among ultra-achieving women in corporate America (those earning more than $100,000 a year) the childlessness figure rises to 49 percent. In contrast, only 25 percent of high-achieving men are childless at age 40, and this figure falls to 19 percent among ultra-achieving men (those earning more than $200,000 a year).[3]

FOR HIGH-ACHIEVING WOMEN, CHILDLESSNESS IS NOT A CHOICE

The vast majority of these women did not choose to be childless. Looking back to their early twenties, when they graduated college, only 14 percent said they definitely had not wanted children.[4] Indeed, among those women who had children, a significant proportion (24 percent) wanted more than they were able to have.

More than a quarter of all high-achieving women in

the 41–55-year-old age bracket said they would still like to have children, and this figure rises to 31 percent among ultra-achievers. Given the odds against these midlife women bearing children, these responses point to a mother lode of pain and yearning.

HIGH-ACHIEVING WOMEN ARE EXTREMELY UNLIKELY TO HAVE A CHILD AFTER AGE 39

Among high-achieving women aged 41–55, only 1 percent had a first child after age 39. And among ultra-achievers, no one had a first child after age 36. Most of the women in each group who were mothers had their first child in their early or mid-20s.

HIGH-ACHIEVING WOMEN ARE EXTREMELY UNLIKELY TO GET MARRIED AFTER AGE 35

When high-achieving women marry, they tend to marry young. In the older group, only 8 percent got married for the first time after age 30, and only 3 percent after age 35.

FOR WOMEN, IT'S LONELY AT THE TOP

Only 60 percent of high-achieving women in the older age group are currently married, and this figure falls to 57 percent in corporate America.[5] By way of contrast,

76 percent of older men are currently married and this figure rises to 83 percent among ultra-achievers.

AFRICAN-AMERICAN WOMEN FACE AN EVEN MORE DIFFICULT REALITY

Only 33 percent of high-achieving African-American women are currently married and 43 percent have children. In the older age group, (41–55) 48 percent are childless. Indeed, among older African-American women no one had a child after age 37 and no one was married after age 28.[6] Balancing career and family seems to be a particularly difficult challenge for women of color.

THE "SECOND SHIFT" IS ALIVE AND WELL

High-earning women continue to take prime responsibility for home and children. Indeed, 40 percent of high-achieving wives feel that their husbands create more work for them around the house than they contribute.

This is even true for ultra-achieving wives (half of whom are married to men earning less than they do). In these marriages only 8 percent of husbands take prime responsibility for helping children with homework, and a mere 5 percent take prime responsibility for cleaning the house.

HYPE TRUMPS REALITY ON THE
FERTILITY FRONT

Despite the fact that 21 percent of women in the younger age group have experienced fertility problems, 89 percent of young, high-achieving women believe that they will be able to get pregnant into their forties.

IN HIGH-ALTITUDE CAREERS, HOURS AT
WORK ARE LONG AND GETTING LONGER

The more successful the woman, the longer her workweek. Twenty-nine percent of high-achievers and 34 percent of ultra-achievers work more than 50 hours a week (medicine, law, and academia are particularly time-intensive). Among ultra-achievers, a significant minority (14 percent) work more than 60 hours a week. A third of these women work longer hours than they did five years ago.

WOMEN ENTREPRENEURS DO A MUCH
BETTER JOB BALANCING THEIR LIVES
THAN WOMEN IN CORPORATE AMERICA

Self-employed, high-achieving women are much less likely to be childless than women who work in corporate America (22 percent versus 42 percent in the older age group). This gap widens even further among ultra-achievers (22 percent versus 49 percent). Self-employed women are also more likely to be married than women in corporate America (67 percent versus 57 percent).

YOUNGER WOMEN FACE EVEN HARDER CHOICES

The tough trade-offs faced by breakthrough-generation women dog the footsteps of younger women. Indeed, if you compare women in the younger age group with women in the older age group by calculating what proportion had a child by age 35, younger women seem to be in worse shape. Only 45 percent of younger women have had a child by age 35, while 62 percent of older women had had a child by this point in time. In other words, young women are having a harder time balancing work and family than their older sisters.[7]

HIGH-POTENTIAL WOMEN WHO LEFT THEIR CAREERS WANT TO GET BACK ON TRACK

A large proportion of high-potential women who left their careers when a child was born feel that this decision was forced on them by long workweeks, unsympathetic employers and inflexible workplaces. The majority (66 percent) would like to be back at work.

WORKPLACE POLICIES MAKE A DIFFERENCE

High-achieving mothers who stay in their careers work for companies that offer a rich array of work/life options—flextime, paid leave, reduced hour jobs, etc. In sharp contrast, many high-potential mothers currently not in careers left companies that had much less in the way of work/life policies.

"CHILDFREE" EMPLOYEES OFTEN RESENT PARENT "PERKS"

Fifty-four percent of high-achieving women without children say that in their workplaces people without children are unfairly expected to pick up the slack for those who have children. This rift between working parents and the "childfree" has the potential of becoming ugly.

HIGH-ACHIEVING WOMEN ARE SKEPTICAL ABOUT "HAVING IT ALL"

Only a small proportion of high-achieving women (16 percent) feel that it is very likely that a woman can "have it all" in terms of career and family. Women tend to think men fare better on this front:

39 percent of high-achieving women feel that men can "have it all."

Eye-catching, powerful facts and figures! But before examining the rich array of data contained in this new survey in more detail, I want to backtrack and situate *High-Achieving Women, 2001,* in the research literature.

If you dig deep enough it is possible to uncover ten studies published over a fifteen-year time span that provide at least some data on high-achieving women, marriage, and children.[8] One in particular traces the conflict between work and family all the way back to the early years of the twentieth century. In a 1995 study entitled *Career and Family: College Women Look to the Past,* Harvard economist Claudia Goldin traces the professional and family lives of four cohorts of college women across the past century.[9] Women in cohorts 1 and 2 (graduating in 1910 and 1933) had to choose between family and career; they could not have both. Cohort 3 (graduating between 1946 and 1965) adopted the pattern of "family then job." For these women family came first, in terms of both timing and priority, though once the children were launched they went back to work, generally finding jobs in the pink-collar ghetto. Cohort 4 (graduating between 1966 and 1979) contains a large group of women who sought to pursue both family and professional careers simultaneously. Only a few succeeded. Goldin finds that only a small slice (13–17 percent) of this breakthrough generation managed to achieve both a career and children by the time they turned 40. Indeed, among the women who attained careers, fully 50 percent remained childless.

Claudia Goldin, born in 1946, is herself part of this breakthrough generation. When I interviewed her in October of 1999, she talked eloquently about the "brutal trade-offs" faced by her generation of American women. She was talking about her study, but she was also talking about her own life. The first woman to receive tenure in Economics at Harvard, Goldin is unmarried and childless. She feels she paid a very high price for her career.

To touch on some of the other research: In a 1994 study, Danity Little looks at executive women in public service and attempts to answer the question: How did they make it to the top? Fifty-one percent of these women are childless and 31 percent are unmarried (single, divorced, or separated). In a 1996 book, Deborah Swiss examines the experiences of 325 women who overcame barriers in the workplace to achieve success across a wide range of careers. Forty percent of these women are childless and 35 percent are unmarried. And a much more recent study of MBA graduates—published by Catalyst in 2000—finds that women MBAs are much more likely than men to be childless (45 percent versus 34 percent) and unmarried (31 percent versus 20 percent).[10]

The studies described above and in the endnotes are richly suggestive. Across a range of professions, high-achieving women continue to have an exceedingly hard time combining career and family. Depending on which study you look at, somewhere between 34 percent and 61 percent of high-achieving women are childless in midlife.

But these studies are also exceedingly problematic if you're interested in constructing a coherent national picture. The data they provide are fragmentary—one study may look at a particular graduating class, another may look at a specific economic sector. They also tend to be inconsistent—different age groups and base years make the data difficult to combine or compare. In addition, because many of these studies were designed to address specific workplace issues—glass ceilings, gender gaps, discrimination—the data they provide on marriage and children have little range or depth. For example, there is very little information on how the childless women in these studies view motherhood. Had they wanted to have a child? If so, what were the main factors that had prevented them from having one? As I started in on the research that underpins this book it quickly became apparent that if I wanted to understand how professional women feel about the challenges that faced them on the work/family front I needed better data—which is when I decided to design and field *High-Achieving Women, 2001*.

It's now time to explore its findings in greater depth. My intention here is to link the data to the voices of the women—and men—who participated in the *High-Achieving Women, 2001* survey. Many of the respondents expressed a willingness to do a follow-up interview—either by phone or by e-mail—and in the weeks immediately after fielding the survey I either talked with, or wrote to, some 50 individuals. The resulting vignettes are quite different from the stories presented in chapter 1. Unlike the women featured there—many of whom are prominent, high-earning individuals—the women who participated in the survey are "regular" professionals, selected because they are representative of the top 10 percent of women across the country. This is not such a rarefied group. Remember that in the older age group (the breakthrough generation) it comprises a sample of women who earn more than $65,000 a year, and in the younger age group it comprises a sample who earn more than $55,000 a year. It should also be borne in mind that unlike the elaborate, extended interviews of chapter 1, these vignettes are based on interviews that were quite short and the women are not identified. An underlying condition of the survey was that the participants would remain anonymous. With these caveats, my hope is that these new voices will allow the facts and figures contained in *High-Achieving Women, 2001* to come alive.

Baby Hunger

Sarah, 45, works as an account manager for a large, Atlanta-based insurance company. We talked about her evolving view of childlessness:

> Up until last year I was in denial. If anyone asked me whether I wanted children I would stare them in the eye, answer an emphatic no, and snow them with stories about how great my life was. I would describe my exciting job and my exotic vacations and talk enthusiastically about being "unencumbered"—a word I've always liked a lot. Then, last summer, my much younger sister had a baby and baby hunger hit me like a ton of bricks. I found it excruciatingly painful to even be around my brand-new niece. One of the few times I held little Lucy she rooted around in my neck and as I felt her unbelievably soft, newborn skin the physical craving to hold my own baby became almost unbearable.
>
> This whole experience stirred me up. I guess I was forced to recognize that children are a big deal, that I had missed out on something huge.

The thoughts and feelings of Sarah are close to the center of gravity of this book. As we learned from the survey at the beginning of the chapter, *33 percent of older high-achieving women are childless, and this figure rises to 42 percent in corporate America*—precisely where Sarah works. The survey also tells us that there is considerable variation between occupations. Among female academics (professors and other high-level educators) the childlessness rate is relatively high (43 percent), while among female entrepreneurs, the childlessness rate is relatively low (22 percent).

There is even more variation among ultra-achieving women—those earning more than $100,000 a year. At these high altitudes, corporate women do particularly badly (49 percent are childless), entrepreneurs do particularly well (22 percent are childless), while doctors and lawyers are somewhere in between.

And, as the survey points out, for many of these women, childlessness is not a preferred outcome. In *High-Achieving Women, 2001* we asked the question: Please think back to when you graduated from college. What did you imagine your life would be like in the future? Did you want children? *Only 14 percent said they very likely would not have children.* In other words, for high-achieving women there is a huge gap between their "reality" and their "dream."

It is also true that large numbers of breakthrough-generation women have fewer children than they had wanted. Back when they graduated from college, only 8 percent of these women said they wanted one child, the majority wanted two (55 percent), and a sizable minority wanted three (17 percent). In the event, *32 percent of these older, high-achieving women had just one child.* For many, this is a source of deep regret.

Sonia, 46, a research scientist at the University of Chicago, talked about her failed attempt to have a second child:

> We had our first child when I was thirty-six years old. It was a completely normal pregnancy, and we were thrilled when our son was born. I remember feeling pleased that we had timed things so well. Delaying this first child until after I had completed my Ph.D. and was settled in my career seemed like such a smart thing to do. Three years later I got pregnant with our second child—and miscarried in the tenth week. I was enormously upset, but not devastated. I thought it would just be a matter of months before I was pregnant again. It never happened. We spent four years in and out of infertility treatment, but nothing worked. When we finally gave up, I plunged into a deep depression from which I am only just recovering.
>
> If only I had realized earlier on how fiercely I wanted that second child—not just for me, but for my husband and son.

There are three of us who meet at a nearby health club Saturday mornings. Three women, each with one precious child. The pretense is exercise but we really meet to grieve. We sit in the juice bar and talk—and weep—and talk some more.

Our stories are different. One woman is married to a much older man who doesn't want a second child. The other woman is in her early forties and newly divorced. But we share this aching loss around children we will never have.

It sounds crazy, doesn't it? How can an imagined child provoke such deep grief?

Part of it is we all have much-loved older children and know what we are missing.

High-achieving men do not experience a significant gap between what they want and what they have on the children front. There is very little discrepancy between their "reality" and their "dream" in terms of ability to have children—79 percent wanted children, 75 percent have children. It's also true that the vast majority of these accomplished men have more than one child. Sixteen percent have one child, 46 percent have two children, and the rest (38 percent) have more than two.

Men also have time on their side. As we shall see in chapter 5, for women, age 40 pretty much marks the end of the childbearing years, while men have many more years to "father" a child if they so desire.

In an open-ended question in the survey, older, child-less, high-achieving women were invited to say why they didn't have children. They cited a variety of reasons: 19 percent pointed to infertility problems; 13 percent said they had not found a partner and did not want to raise a child alone; 13 percent said that their husbands did not want a child.

Cara, 46, a musician with a San Francisco-based chamber orchestra, is thoroughly in touch with the veto power of an unwilling husband.

> In my early forties, with baby hunger peaking, I decided that I could not wait for Mr. Right any longer, and that I should just go ahead and adopt a Chinese baby on my own.
>
> Well, I was fairly far along—I had completed a home study and was halfway through the mountain of red tape that accompanies any adoption—when Frank walked into my life. We fell in love and a few weeks later he moved in with me. I was over the moon. After twenty-five years of failed relationships I had finally found the man of my dreams. But Frank came with strings attached. He had just turned fifty-five and already had three grown children by his first wife. He most definitely did not want a baby. For him it was a deal breaker. He sat me down and said as gently and firmly as he knew how, "I would like for us to get married but this won't happen unless you put

away those videos of cute, Chinese babies forever."
I cried and felt sorry for myself but in the end I
signed on to his deal and last summer we were
married. Most of the time I think I made the right
decision.

The Face of Marriage

Annette, 42, is a partner at a Washington, D.C., law
firm. She is also happily married, but feels strongly that
she wouldn't be if she'd tried to develop both her
career and a relationship simultaneously.

> I didn't get married until I was twenty-seven, but
> I married someone I had been living with for five
> years. In fact, Tom and I met when we were in
> high school and started dating when we were col-
> lege sophomores. By the time we made it to the
> altar, we had been seriously involved for ten years.
>   Looking back, I feel I was very lucky. The col-
> lege years are great years to connect with some-
> one. It's about the only time in life you can spend
> a whole weekend talking. You kind of establish
> the trust—and build up the IOUs—for the tough
> years ahead. At least for me, the years from age
> twenty-four to thirty-four were a blur. First there
> was law school, and then there were seven brutal
> years as an associate when I worked twelve- to
> fourteen-hour days. It wasn't until I made partner
> that I was able to come up for air.

If I hadn't met Tom early on I'm not sure I
would have married. I look at my single friends
and marvel at how difficult it is to nurture a
"beginning" relationship when your career is
going full throttle.

As we learned from the survey, only *60 percent of
breakthrough-generation women are currently married,* and this figure falls to 57 percent in corporate
America. Again, there is variation between occupations. Sixty-nine percent of women entrepreneurs in
the 41–55 age group are currently married, but this figure falls to 51 percent for women in the professions
(lawyers and doctors), and to 45 percent for women in
academe.

Overall, high-achieving women are much less likely
than their male counterparts to be married. Three-
quarters (76 percent) of high-achieving men in the
41–55 age group are currently married. This figure
falls slightly—to 70 percent—for men in the professions. High-achieving women are also more likely to be
divorced or separated (18 percent) than high-achieving
men (12 percent).

When high-achieving women marry, they marry
young. Seventy-five percent of married women in the
older age group (41–55) got married for the first time
before they were 24. Only 8 percent got married for the
first time after age 30, and only 3 percent after age 35.

High-achieving women tend to marry highly successful men. Nine out of ten high-achieving women (89 percent) are married to men who are employed full-time or are self-employed, and a quarter are married to men who earn over $100,000 a year. Indeed, only 14 percent of the husbands earn less than $35,000 a year. In sharp contrast, only 39 percent of high-achieving men are married to women who are employed full-time, and 40 percent of these wives earn less than $35,000 a year. It seems that these men often marry women who are less career driven than they are. At least some of the younger, high-achieving women who participated in the survey felt that men were very easily threatened by their accomplishments. In the words of Leah, a 28-year-old law student:

> I can't believe it. I'm becoming one of those
> women who scare men. I mean me—the girl with
> the freckles and the tattoo. I began to notice it last
> fall when I started at NYU. At about the same
> time I met this guy who's a second-year student at
> Brooklyn Law. We went out on a couple of dates
> but from the get-go it was clear that he hated that
> the outside world saw "my" place as better than
> 'his' place. Who cares? I surely don't. But he kept
> on bringing it up, and then it became an issue.
> After a few weeks of snide, silly remarks about my
> status school, I said "forget this" and we broke up.
> It was a pity. I liked him a lot.

High-Altitude Careers

Marilyn, 33, an executive with a Boston-based advertising company, has an interesting intergenerational take on the workweek.

> When I was growing up, my dad was an executive in the advertising industry. He worked for a much smaller company, but that difference aside, I have a very similar job to the one he had at my age. Well, Dad couldn't type, nor did he like to place his own phone calls, so when his secretary went home at 5:00 P.M. he became totally dysfunctional—he didn't even pretend to do any work until she reappeared at 9:00 A.M. the next morning. When I was ten years old, I remember him joking around, telling my mom that this was why he needed dinner on the table at six o'clock sharp.
>
> I often think of the difference between his workday and my workday. It's not just that I spend many more hours at the office—that's a given these days. I am also hooked into a technology that allows work to seep into every cranny of my life. I have a computer and a fax machine in my office and at home, I have voice mail in the office, on my cell phone, and at home, I have e-mail in the office and at home, and my boss has just given me a Blackberry so I can check my e-mail on the hour every hour wherever I am!
>
> When I answered the question on the survey

about total hours worked in an average week, I
wrote down 56. This seemed like a solid figure
and it does capture my 10-hour day at the office
and the hour I spend on e-mail each evening at
home. But it doesn't reflect the true load. The
requirement that I be constantly in touch makes
me anxious and preoccupied a great deal of the
time. I don't think I ever tune out and switch off
the way my father did every day of the week.[11]

High-Achieving Women, 2001 tells us that 29 percent of
high-achieving women work the kind of hours Marilyn
works—over 50 hours a week. The more successful
you are, the longer the workweek. Thirty-four percent
of ultra-achievers work over 50 hours a week, and the
professional fields of medicine, law, and academia seem
to be particularly time-intensive.

Across occupation and sector, high-achieving women
are working considerably harder than they were even a
few years ago. For example, almost a third of high
achievers work more than they did five years ago, and
of these, a quarter work 20 hours more per week than
they used to. Among ultra-achievers, a third work more
than they did five years ago, and of these, more than a
third work 20 hours more per week than they used to.
A quarter of all ultra-achievers are away from home on
a business trip at least five nights every three months.

Many of the respondents in our survey—men, as well as women—resented the work pressures in their lives.

John, 37, who works for a graphic design company in Cambridge, Massachusetts, sees the long-hours culture as inefficient—and unfair.

> I'd like to see evening and weekend work go back to being the exception, not the expectation, for employees. Working hard doesn't mean that everyone needs to work longer hours. You can work smart, utilize technology, leverage assistance within your division, and be out the door at 5:30, but that's frowned upon in today's office environment. You definitely need to put in a whole lot of "face" time particularly in the evening, which is a real killer if you have a family.

The Second Shift

High-achieving women continue to carry the lion's share of domestic responsibilities. Fifty percent of married, high-achieving women assume prime responsibility for meal preparation—only 9 percent of their husbands/partners take prime responsibility for this task.[12] Fifty-six percent of these women take prime responsibility for doing the laundry; only 10 percent of husbands take care of this task. And 45 percent of women make sure the house is cleaned; only 5 percent of husbands take care of this task. Younger wives do slightly less than older wives, and younger husbands do slightly more than older husbands, indicating that the division of labor has become slightly more equal over the years. However, these shifts have been quite small. To pick one example, 8 percent of older husbands take care of the laundry, compared to 13 percent of younger husbands.

At the end of the day, the division of labor on the home front boils down to one startling fact: *43 percent percent of older, high-achieving women, and 37 percent of younger, high-achieving women feel that their husbands create more work for them around the house than they contribute*. Thirty-nine percent of ultra-achieving women also feel this way, despite the fact that half the women in this group are married to men who earn less than they do. As might be expected, the unequal load at home can be the source of marital tension.

Deborah, 37, lives in St. Paul, Minnesota, and is president of a small publishing company. She talked about her feelings:

I loved the question about husbands creating more work than they contribute. Don't I have one of those! Dan's a wonderful man, but enormously difficult to live with. I know which room he has spent time in because he leaves behind a trail of discarded stuff—beer bottles, coffee mugs, wet towels, dental floss, junk mail, you name it. He tells me he doesn't really "see" disorder or mess, which is why he doesn't get around to picking any of it up.

If I ask him to do something specific, he'll do it, but so badly that I generally have to do it over. When he clears the table he is very likely to dump all the dishes in the sink rather than empty the dishwasher and put the dirty dishes where they need to be. When he does the grocery shopping he refuses to use a list—he thinks lists are annoying—so invariably I have to go back to the store and pick up the things he forgot. And it's not as though any of these problems are new. For thirteen years I've tried to find a way of changing his behavior—I've wheedled, I've cajoled, I've threatened, I've staged temper tantrums. But nothing works, it's like water on a duck's back.

Back in the days when he was under more work pressure than I was, I didn't mind so much—picking up after him, doing the lion's share of the housework. But now that I earn more than he does—and work longer hours—it drives me crazy. His latest excuse is, "You can't teach an old dog new tricks." Give me a break! Is that supposed to make me feel better?

When it comes to responsibility for children, husbands don't do much better. *High-Achieving Women, 2001* tells us that only 9 percent of husbands take time off from work when a child is sick, while the figure is 48 percent for their high-achieving wives. Eight percent of husbands take prime responsibility for helping children with homework, compared to 39 percent of wives. And 3 percent of these husbands organize activities such as play dates and summer camp, compared to 58 percent of their wives.

Wasted Potential

"I replay it in my head at least three times a week," Marcia told me wistfully. "Could I have handled things differently?"

Marcia, 53, was talking about a decision she made 18 years ago to give up a job as dean of the faculty at a liberal arts college in Westchester County.

At the time it seemed as though I had no choice. IBM decided to relocate my husband to Austin just before my second child was born, so I resigned my job and all four of us moved to Texas. Of course, I had no idea that I would never again get within shooting distance of such a wonderful job.

Now with the girls "launched" I would give my eyeteeth to have something substantial to sink my teeth into. And it's not for want of trying. Over the last five years I must have applied for forty or fifty jobs, but all I've been able to come up with is

this little job in the admissions office of the local
private school—which uses perhaps a tenth of my
skills and energy.

Recent data from the Census Bureau shows that fully 22
percent of women with professional degrees (MBAs,
M.D.s, Ph.D.s and the like) are currently not in the paid
labor force.[13] The reasons are fairly obvious. *High-
Achieving Women, 2001* demonstrates that large numbers of talented women are forced out of their careers
when they have children. Furthermore, the survey shows
that 66 percent of these high-potential women would like
to be back in full time work on a career track.

These women are highly educated and have impressive resumes. Five percent left jobs in which they were
the CEO of an organization, and more than a third (40
percent) left jobs in which they were one or two report-
ing levels away from the CEO slot. The majority of
these women left their careers when their first or second
child was born. Fully 45 percent feel that their decision
to leave full-time employment was forced on them by
long workweeks. Another 40 percent blame unsympathetic managers who failed to provide or encourage
the use of work/life policies—flextime, paid or unpaid
leave, childcare, etc. Maureen is a case in point.

When I became pregnant with Deborah, I
was working as the development director of a

museum in Brooklyn. I was thirty-seven years
old with a history of miscarriage, so my then-boss
said it would be okay if I cut back my hours a little. But three months into the pregnancy he was
fired and my new boss was much more rigid. She
required that I work a fifty-hour week, plus, she
slapped on some extra travel. It was a mess. I
went into labor in the seventh month, gave birth
to a premature baby, and then took several
months off work, which is when they replaced
me. I guess I could have fought to get my job
back, I think I was legally entitled, but at the time
it didn't seem worth it. I was dealing with a 3-
pound baby and a two-hourly feeding schedule.
In retrospect, it seems ironic that part of the mission of the museum was celebrating family life
through the ages.

   It was a mistake—not to fight for that job.
Deborah is now five years old and this last winter
I hit the job market. I am finding the pickings
extremely slim. I am beginning to realize that I
may never replicate the job I lost.

Maureen is not alone in believing that her pregnancy
triggered shabby treatment in the workplace. The survey found that many high-potential women currently
not in careers left organizations with inadequate
work/life policies. In contrast, high-achieving women

currently on-track in their careers tend to work for organizations that offer substantial help to working mothers. Flextime, telecommuting, reduced-hour schedules, paid parenting leave, compressed work-weeks, and help with childcare are all much more likely to be part of the benefits package at these organizations.

High-achieving women who are on-track in their careers feel strongly that not only do their workplaces offer a rich array of work/life policies, but their managers encourage people to use them; almost 90 percent of the women surveyed said they have made personal use of one of these policies. In sharp contrast, only 7 percent of high-potential women—those who left their careers mostly for family reasons—feel that managers in their previous place of work had encouraged the use of work/life policies.

It seems that work/life policies pay off. Companies that offer a generous array of options are much more likely to retain high-achieving women when they become mothers. Among other things, this means that these firms do not incur the heavy costs associated with replacing professional employees, but more on this issue in chapter 6, which deals with workplace policy.

Lessons for Younger Women

High-Achieving Women, 2001 contains some good news for young women. Women in the younger age group (28–40) feel able to be considerably more ambitious than women in the older age group (41–55). When they graduated college, 67 percent of the younger women expected to hold an executive position (compared with 56 percent of older women), and fully 83 percent expected to earn a high salary (compared to 71 percent of older women).

As I pointed out earlier, younger women are also less likely than older women to be responsible for household chores. Doing the laundry is a case in point. Only 47 percent of younger women take prime responsibility for this task, compared to 63 percent of older women.

The news on the childbearing front is much less encouraging.

High-Achieving Women, 2001 tells us that only 40 percent of younger, high-achieving women have children, and this figure falls to 34 percent among young African American women. The difficulties young, white women face on the work/family front, seem to be more severe for young, black women.

Clearly, many of these younger women risk not having children at all. The median age for the group is 34, which does not bode well for their chances. *High-Achieving Women, 2001* demonstrates that when high-achieving women do have children, they tend to have them in their twenties or very early thirties. The data from the survey show that among older women, the most popular age to have a first child was 22, while among younger women the most popular age—so far—is 29. (See Figure 1.)

Figure 1

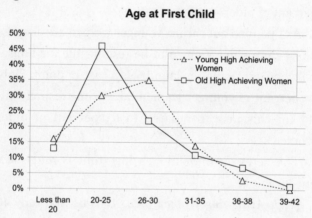

Age at First Child

Perhaps large numbers of younger women are pinning their hopes on ART and expect to have a child down the road when they are 38 or 40. After all, *High-Achieving Women, 2001* tells us that 89 percent of these women believe that ART will allow them to get pregnant deep into their forties. Take Amy, for example.

Amy, 29, earns $29,000 a year as a Minneapolis-based yoga instructor. Her income does not qualify her for inclusion in *High-Achieving Women, 2001;* she snuck in by virtue of her magna cum laude degree from Stanford University. Through an e-mail, Amy shared her long-range plans.

> I figure I've got fourteen, fifteen years before I need worry about making babies—and boy, doesn't that take the pressure off! My plan is to stay with yoga for another few years. I love it and it's beginning to give me the opportunity to travel—I'm heading up a workshop in Bali next month. Then, sometime in my mid-30s, I'll go back to school, earn an MBA, and get myself a serious career—maybe it'll even be yoga-related. Which brings me to forty. At that point, I'll be ready for marriage and family. I can't tell you how glad I am that this new reproductive technology virtually guarantees that you can have a baby up until forty-five. Or maybe it's even later. It seems that every time I pick up the paper there's another medical breakthrough. Go, doctors!

Amy's relaxed take on childbearing might work out. But then again, it might not. *High-Achieving Women, 2001* shows us that late-in-life children are extremely rare. Only 1 percent of the women in the 41–55 age group had a first child after age 39. Among African-

American women no one had a child after 37, and among ultra-achieving women, no one had a first child after age 36. Indeed, in all categories, most of the older women who became mothers had their first child in their twenties. As we shall see from the evidence presented in chapter five, the chances of Amy getting pregnant in her early forties are tiny—somewhere in the 3–5 percent range.

If she delays settling down until age 40, she might also have trouble finding a husband. In this area *High-Achieving Women, 2001* has some discouraging findings. Older high-achieving women who married, tended to marry young. Overall, only 8 percent got married for the first time after age 30, and only 3 percent after age 35. Among older African-American women the situation is even more extreme. In this group no one got married after the age of 28.

Thus, a pattern of "if you get married you get married young" seems to be repeating itself in the younger age group. To date, 54 percent of all marriages in the younger set happened before age 24. Indeed, there were more marriages between 20 and 24 than between 25 and 29.

The story, however, is far from over: Young high-achieving women still have time and opportunity on their side. What I urge them to do is pay attention to what happened to their older counterparts. Understanding that a large proportion of older high-achieving women missed out on husbands and children and are now deeply regretful might well make for more proactive behavior. In a recent commencement address at Villanova University, the writer Anna Quindlen was extremely persuasive on the point:

> It's so much easier to write a resume than to craft a spirit. But a resume is cold comfort on a winter's night, or when you're sad, or broke or lonely, or when you've gotten back test results and they're not so good.
>
> Here is my resume: I am a good mother to my three children. I am a good friend to my husband. I have tried to make marriage vows mean what they say. I am a good friend to my friends and they to me. Without them, there would be nothing to say to you today, because I would be a cardboard cutout. But I call them on the phone, and I meet them for lunch. I show up. I listen.
>
> I would be rotten, or at least mediocre, at my job, if those other things were not true. You cannot really be first-rate at your work if work is all you are. So here's what I wanted to tell you today: get a life. A real life, not a manic pursuit of the next promotion, the bigger paycheck, the larger house. Do you think you'd care so very much about those things if you blew an aneurysm one afternoon, or found a lump in your breast?

"Having It All": Myth or Reality

The survey tells us that only a small proportion of high-achieving women—16 percent, to be precise—feel that it's very likely that women can "have it all" in terms of career and family. The women interviewed are painfully aware of the obstacles and hurdles, but they also seem resigned to the fact that sacrifice might be a necessary part of a woman's life. Like Lyssa Dent in Wendy Wasserstein's play *An American Daughter,* they feel that public opinion is very grudging, that accomplished women are often seen as "wanting too much" or "having too much."

In the follow-up interviews and e-mails, many high-achieving women without children—particularly in the older group—were bitter and angry when they responded to the question of whether they thought women could "have it all." The following excerpts from several e-mail exchanges illustrate their feelings:

HAVING YOUR CAKE AND EATING IT
TOO. STUPID QUESTION!

I don't use this phrase, I think it is nonsense. You can't have "all" of anything. Some aspect of your life will be compromised in at least some small way while you are focusing on another aspect of life.

It's a pipe dream! Even a superwoman can't find that many hours in the day.

Most people think this means that you don't have
to sacrifice—wrong!!!! To me it means you are
willing to make sacrifices/exchanges for those
things which are important to you!

Finally, there are the men. Strangely enough, the survey tells us that high-achieving men are even more
skeptical about the chances of "having it all" than high-
achieving women. Only 7 percent of male respondents
feel that men can have it all. This unexpected finding
prompted me to conduct a few follow-up interviews
with men who took part in the survey.

Craig is a 53-year-old physician who lives in
Portland, Oregon, and is impressively self-aware.

On paper it looks as though I have it all: a successful career, a long-standing marriage, three beautiful daughters, but if I'm honest, that's not how I
feel.

There were twenty years in there—from the
time I finished medical school to when I resigned
my hospital appointment—when I was so tethered
to my work that I hardly saw my family. The girls
were asleep when I got home at night and on
weekends I was so bone tired I had very little
good energy for them. Thinking back on it, I
know I didn't have children the way my wife had
children. I didn't get to take them out for hot
chocolate after school or hang out with their
friends. To this day I have no idea what music

they like or whether they're afraid of death. I see
this as a permanent loss, the price I paid for an
absorbing career.

Very few people it seems—men or women—manage to
completely escape the trade-offs that reverberate
through this book: between love and work, between
career and children. But if high-altitude careers
inevitably exact a price, it's profoundly unfair that the
highest prices—by far!—are paid by women. Craig
seems like a sensitive, thoughtful guy, and I'm sorry
that he didn't see much of his children when they were
growing up. But let's get real. Craig's not having it all
is an entirely different kettle of fish than Sarah or
Cara's not having it all. Sarah and Cara are childless,
while Craig has three beautiful daughters. He at least
has the possibility of deepening his relationship with
his adult daughters—and becoming the world's best
grandfather.

3

HIGH-ALTITUDE CAREERS
AND THE "PRICE" OF
MOTHERHOOD

I WAS INTRODUCED TO LISA POLSKY by an economist friend in the fall of 1999. At that time she was working at Morgan Stanley, the Wall Street investment banking firm. Polsky was known as a senior woman who often held out a helping hand to younger colleagues, and I was particularly interested in her story. She had, after all, made it on Wall Street—the ultimate bastion of male market power.

Over a several-month period we lunched—hurriedly—at the Century Club and talked over Evian water in her office. I felt as though I was "stealing" chunks of time in her incredibly busy life.

Polsky grew up in rural Pennsylvania and recalls a

happy childhood as the middle child among five brothers and sisters. After high school she attended New
York University, graduated with a degree in business
studies, and went to work for Citibank, where she
helped establish a derivatives division before moving
on to Bankers Trust. Her big break came in 1995 when
she was offered a position at Morgan Stanley as
Managing Director.

Unbeknownst to her new employer, Polsky's big
break triggered the most agonized soul-searching of her
life.

> I got the job offer from Morgan Stanley a month
> before my fortieth birthday, explained Polsky. In
> all kinds of ways this offer was the culmination of
> a fifteen-year work effort and I knew it wasn't in
> me to turn it down, yet I also knew that if I took it
> I would never have a child. The clock was ticking
> and I was running out of time. But how could I, in
> good conscience, think I could deal with this new
> job and a new baby? It simply would not be fair to
> the child. I was going into a higher-stress environ-
> ment—more volatile and more transaction driven
> —and the hours would be brutal. Getting in early
> to follow the markets in Asia and Europe would
> turn my ten-hour day into a fourteen-hour day. I
> remember having these strange conflicting emo-
> tions. I felt torn apart by the decision, but at the

same time I felt robbed of any real choice in the matter.

In our conversations we talked about many issues—the ongoing disparity between male and female earnings in top jobs, the importance of mentors and old girls networks. We even talked about inflation fears and where interest rates were going. But we always returned to "the child I never had" theme. Polsky was 44 and knew that her childbearing days were over.

> What gnaws at me is that I always assumed I would have children—I'm someone who loves kids. In my twenties I put real energy into finding the right man and getting married so that I could have children in the right context. I did get married, but children still eluded me. Somehow I imagined having a child was something I would get to in a year or so, after the next promotion, when I was more established. I just wasn't able to grab the golden ring.

There was more than a hint of grief in her voice as she mused over her decisions, but after allowing me to see her pain, Polsky would invariably pull back and carefully correct any impression I might have that she was complaining.

> Look, I have this wonderful, exhilarating job, and the decision not to have a child was my call. I just

didn't want to be a bad mother. I'm not blaming
anyone.[1]

Those conversations with Lisa Polsky stuck in my
mind. In the first place, I found her decision not to have
a child a courageous one. Given the fact she had a
high income—not to mention a husband—it would
have been easy for her to pursue a more self-indulgent
route by having a child and then turning its care and
upbringing over to others. But Polsky, to her credit,
seemed to anticipate a much more rigorous kind of
motherhood. I was also intrigued by the fact that her
decision-making at age 40 was the opposite of my own.

As I mentioned in the preface, in the mid-1980s I
held a job as executive director of the Economic Policy
Council (EPC), a Manhattan-based think tank that
publishes reports on the outstanding policy issues of the
day. It was a wonderful job, but it was also extremely
pressured. Indeed, it became more stressful over the
years as I developed new projects and expanded the
funding base. By 1986 it was clear to me that this
high-profile job was increasingly incompatible with
fulfilling the needs of my then-small children. So I
quit. A week before my fortieth birthday I just walked
in and told my boss that I felt split in two and needed
to go home and look after my children. At the time I
tried to focus on the positives. After all, I had a lot to be
grateful for. I had three beautiful children and a gem of

a husband who was able to support all five of us. I even had some at-home work possibilities—I could build on the success of my last book and fashion a career as a freelance writer.

But as I went about the transition to at-home mom as cheerfully and energetically as I knew how—hanging out with my children, fixing up the house—I found I needed to fight down feelings of disappointment and failure. This was the second career I had been forced out of, and at age 39 it was impossible to pretend that I could count on a third. Part of me was deeply bereft. I had loved college teaching, and I had adored being a policy wonk. Not so much for the money or the status (there was rather little of either), but because I was committed to the substance of what I did. My passion—as a teacher and as a policy analyst—was to infuse economic policy-making with values I cared about, values that centered on social justice and equal opportunity. It was thus extremely painful to walk away. I was relinquishing the "perks" of an on-track career—salary, colleagues, structure—but, even more important, I felt I was relinquishing some small chance of making a difference.

But I knew what I had to do. My children—particularly three-year-old Adam—needed me. So I went home, regrouped, and started a new existence as a hands-on mom and part-time career person. I worked odd hours, traveled only rarely, and saw a great deal of my children. Like Lisa Polsky, I felt a great deal of clarity about the decisions I needed to make, but this fact did not make the sacrifices less real or less hurtful.

The demands and constraints of modern-day, high-maintenance careers go a long way toward explaining two phenomena: why so many high-achieving women remain childless; and the flip side of the coin, why so many high-potential women are forced off the career ladder once they have children. Some drop out completely, others become crabs—inching sideways, stopping and starting as they repeatedly reinvent their careers so as to better meet the needs of their children.

Let's start at the beginning with young women in their twenties. Established professionals are quite clear in their advice to this new generation: Postpone childbearing as long as you can and there will be, in the words of Felice Schwartz, founder of Catalyst, "a huge payoff in the workplace."[2] According to Lisa Benenson, former editor in chief of *Working Woman* and *Working Mother* magazines, "The signals are very clear. Young women are told that a serious person needs to commit to her career in her twenties and devote all of her energies to her job for at least ten years if she is to be successful."[3]

Distressingly, this expert advice is extremely sound: Motherhood does derail and destroy careers and needs to be avoided if a young woman wants to get a career off the ground in an optimal fashion. This is due to the convergence of two factors. A successful career, particularly in its early stages, is extraordinarily demanding these days. Rigorous professional training, 50–70 hour workweeks, business travel, and stressful work environments all contribute to the load carried by ambitious young women. If they also intend to have children, their lives are further complicated by an extremely inadequate set of supports. At least in America, government and employers do such a poor job supporting working mothers—providing little in the way of paid parenting leave, job-back guarantees, flextime, or quality childcare—that women routinely become downwardly mobile in the labor market once they have children. Two recent studies lay out in very specific terms the economic penalties attached to becoming a mother. Columbia University economist Jane Waldfogel finds that mothers earn less than other women even when you control for marital status, experience and education. In fact, she finds that one child produces a wage "penalty" of 6 percent of earnings while two children produce a wage penalty of 13 percent. In another study, economists Michelle Budig and Paula England find that motherhood produces a penalty of 7 percent per child.[4]

Enormously demanding workweeks and the scarcity of family supports make combining career and family a truly daunting prospect. Young, ambitious women quickly figure out the real deal. "Where I work, super-mom is dead," Karen Maguire told me flatly. "I mean, I don't see anyone doing it." In the fall of 2000, Maguire, 28, was working as an associate in the municipal securities department at Paine Webber. She put in seventy-two-hour weeks and barely had time to wash her hair. "Getting a life," let alone acquiring a husband and children, seemed like an impossible dream.

We arranged to meet for brunch one Saturday in October. Maguire was late. She bounced into the restaurant, long hair flying, breathless, and full of apologies. She explained that the previous evening she had gotten together with some of her "guy" friends from college. It was a rare event and she had savored it. But it had turned into an exceedingly late night and it had been hard getting out of bed.

Maguire had given a great deal of thought to the work/family challenge and over French toast and strawberries launched into a theory she described as "backward mapping."

"Women like me like to do this backward mapping," she said, "which means starting with what you want and working backwards. The problem is that the time frames don't fit together."

Take my situation. If I want to have two or three children—and I do—and if I am not prepared to use fancy reproductive engineering (being Catholic, I think I will go the natural way) I need to think about having my last child in my early forties.

I then start backing up, leaving two or three years in between each child, and this pushes me to my mid-thirties. This is when I would need to have a first child. So then I think, okay, if I need to be married and ready to have a child by the age of 35, I need to find a husband soon—I mean, it takes a while to meet a guy and then there is at least a couple of years between meeting and marriage.

I go through this exercise and then I think of my job and I start laughing. I mean, it's a joke. When am I going to do all this? Right now I have so little time to meet men that I have started using an Internet dating service. And even that isn't working too well. I don't begin to have enough "search time" or "relationship maintenance" time.

Maguire is an extremely well-organized young person who doesn't like having so little control over her life. With degrees from the University of Chicago and the Kennedy School at Harvard University, she had originally planned to work in government. But as she put it, "The big financial firms kind of suck you in."

They make an offer pretty early on in the recruiting process before you know about any other kind
of job, and the money's so good it's hard to turn
them down. So here I am, earning six figures at a
big-time, private-sector job.

I try hard to rein in my lifestyle. I live in a
walk-up over a kosher barbecue on West 72nd
Street in a strange, goofy apartment which is a lot
cheaper than the "doorman with health club" deal
most of my friends opt for. But I don't kid myself.
To move to a government job I would need to take
a two-thirds pay cut and that would be hard.

My schedule is unreal. I usually get to work
around nine, except for Mondays when we have
an 8:00 o'clock meeting. And usually I stay until
10:00 or 10:30 P.M. I also put in several hours on
Sundays. What happens is that during the regular
day I do the work that requires contact with other
people. And in the evenings and on Sundays I do
the work that has been dumped on me by my various bosses. Evenings and weekends tend to be
pure execution.

Dinner during the week is always take-out. I
have this joke that I know the weather based on
the clothing of the delivery person. If he's wearing
a T-shirt I know it's warm outside. I work in a
cubicle under fluorescent lights in the center of the
building and rarely see the outside world.

I used to think that if I gave this job my all

for, say, seven years, things would ease up a bit.
But I don't think so anymore. The people I know
who've been here for seven years are still at the
vice president level and they're still proving themselves. They're like the key support staff who
make it happen for the guy who's really in charge.
They're at his beck and call and their hours are as
bad as mine.

Ten, twelve years out, at the first vice president
level, things begin to change. At this point you
have the knowledge and contacts to generate business, and if you become a substantial rainmaker
you do eventually earn a little flexibility and independence—you could take a few liberties without
getting fired.

The problem is, of course, that in ten, twelve
years I will be 38 or 40, and that's not the time to
begin thinking about finding a husband or having
children. It's way off the map.

I asked Maguire whether the guys in her office sat
around doing "backward mapping" exercises.

She almost choked on her orange juice.

"That will be the day," she spluttered. And, as she
described the lives of her immediate colleagues, it
became clear that the problems she was facing were
extremely gender specific.

Half of the male associates in my group—the
municipal securities group—are already married

with children. And in all cases they have stay-at-home wives. In contrast, most of the female associates are single. Only two of them are married and neither have children.

Further up the career ladder the male/female divide becomes even more marked as the number of women drops off. Half of the associates, but only a quarter of the vice presidents, are women, and men increasingly acquire families while women do not.

Men on the rungs above me have a wife, kids, one or two houses, the works. The associates and vice presidents live in New Jersey and the managing directors live in Connecticut. Otherwise they are carbon copies. The thing I don't see is senior women having rich family lives. There are just two forty-something women in my group whom I see as role models careerwise. One is divorced, and the other one—who is super successful—is about to get divorced. Both of these women are childless.

I had one last question for her. "So what are you going to do about your big-time, private sector career?" I asked.

Maguire looked me straight in the eye. "If I want kids, I'll have to bag it," she said.[5]

Lisa Polsky and Karen Maguire are not unusual. In high-pressure, demanding careers, women are having a rough time. They make up a small minority of those who hold "top jobs" and find it extremely difficult to combine family with career. But let's back up and put these stories in a wider context.

Sixty-two million American women are now at work. In 1999 fully 77 percent of women aged 25–54 were in the labor force, up from 57 percent in 1976. Overall, women now make up 47 percent of the American workforce. This enormous expansion in the number of women in paid employment has been accompanied by some real progress in closing the gap between male and female wages. According to the Bureau of Labor Statistics, between 1979 and 1999 the percentage of women's earnings to men's earnings for full-time year-round workers, climbed from 63 percent to 77 percent.[6]

This dramatic narrowing of the wage gap has been the focus of much celebration—and deservedly so. However, little attention has been paid to the fact that for high-achieving women and their male counterparts, the gap remains as entrenched and as stubborn as ever. In 1999 the top 10 percent of women earned an average of $55,000 a year, while the top 10 percent of men earned an average of $87,500. In other words, high-echelon women earn a mere 62 percent of the male wage, and this is despite the fact that there are more women in executive, administrative, and managerial occupations than ever before. In the years between 1989 and 2000, the percentage of women in these top positions rose from 39 percent to 45 percent.[7]

The essential reality is that women are not making it into upper management in significant numbers, and the ones who get there are paid significantly less than their male counterparts. In 2000, women constituted a mere 4 percent of all top corporate earners—defined as the five most highly compensated officers in *Fortune* 1000 companies—and filled only 7 percent of line positions in these companies. (Line positions are those with profit-and-loss responsibility and are generally seen as stepping-stones to the top).[8] According to Sheila Wellington, President of Catalyst, the leading non-profit organization working to advance women in business, "Until more women move into line positions, you won't find women in many corner offices."[9] Indeed, in 1999 only six of the *Fortune* 1000 companies were headed by a woman.

Twenty years ago, business leaders could dismiss these kinds of figures with a wave of the hand as a pipeline problem. Thousands of women were entering the professions; they just hadn't had enough time to make their way up through the hierarchy. It's much harder to make that argument today. For the last twenty or thirty years, manufacturing corporations, banks, law firms, universities, and hospitals have added large numbers of women to their professional workforce—often filling 40–50 percent of entry-level positions with women—but, by and large, have not promoted them. There seems to be a revolving door for women at the bottom of the professional career ladders; they get a foot on the ladder but then either stay put or get pushed off within five to ten years. The law profession is a case in point.

Today, 47 percent of law school students are women, as are 41 percent of the associates in private law firms. Yet only 14 percent of the partners in these firms are women. On law school faculties, women make up 52 percent of assistant professors, but hold only 6 percent of the tenured slots (associate and full professorships).[10]

Not that women have not come a long way. Just over a century ago, in 1873, the United States Supreme Court ruled that a young woman named Myra Bradwell was not constitutionally entitled to practice law. In his opinion, Justice Joseph P. Bradley wrote: "The natural and proper timidity and delicacy which belongs to the female sex evidently unfits it for many of the occupations of civil life. The paramount destiny and mission of women are to fulfill the noble and benign office of wife and mother. This is the law of the Creator."[11] Columbia University did not admit its first woman law student until 1928, and as late as the mid-1960s only 5 percent of the graduating class was female.

One particularly disturbing fact about the contemporary labor market is that American women are doing less well—relative to men—than women in other advanced industrial countries. In a recent study, economists Susan Harkness and Jane Waldfogel compared the wage gap across seven industrialized countries and found it was particularly wide in the United States and the United Kingdom. For example, in France, women earn 81 percent of the male wage, in Australia 88 percent, and in Sweden 84 percent, while in the United States women earn 78 percent and in the United Kingdom 75 percent.[12]

So why are so few American women rising to the top? And why have they made less progress closing in on men than women in other countries?

Children lie at the heart of the matter. Close analysis of today's wage gap reveals that only a small portion of the gap can be attributed to discrimination (getting paid less for doing the same job, or being denied access—to jobs, education, or credit—on account of sex). Increasingly, women earn less than men because of the unequal impact of family responsibilities.

Here is the plotline. Over the last 35 years, most advanced industrial democracies—and most especially the United States—have waged a battle against discrimination, enacting and implementing a variety of equal pay and equal opportunity policies. In the United

States, the Equal Pay Act of 1963; Title VII of the Civil Rights Act, passed in 1964 and amended in 1991 to permit individuals to recover punitive damages if they suffer discrimination, and Title IX of the Education Act of 1972; have been particularly powerful. Discrimination hasn't disappeared, but it has been reduced, and in its more blatant forms now accounts for a relatively small part of the wage gap. According to recent studies, an increasingly large part of the wage gap can be explained by the unequal impact of children on adult lives. Childbearing and child rearing interrupt and limit women's careers, permanently depressing their earning power. If the gap between what men and women earn in the United States is wider than elsewhere, it isn't because this country has done a less good job combating discrimination. Rather, it is due to the fact that the United States has failed to develop policies—in workplaces and in the wider society—that support working mothers. Various kinds of evidence link the wage gap to women's family responsibilities.

Take the pattern of earnings over the life cycle. When women enter the workforce in their early and mid-twenties, they earn almost as much as men do. At ages 25–29 they earn 87 percent of the male wage. For a few years, they keep pace with male earnings. However, when women hit the prime childbearing years, their earnings fall way behind those of men. By ages 40–44, women earn a mere 71 percent of the male wage.[13] In other words, women miss out on the rapid, upward mobility men typically experience in their late twenties and early thirties. At this critical stage in most career paths, a significant proportion of women have children and many are forced to make dramatic compromises in their work lives. Some leave the labor force for a few years, others cut back to part time. In the words of economist Lester Thurow, "The years between 25 and 35 are the prime years for establishing a successful career. These are the years when hard work has the maximum payoff. They are also the prime years for launching a family. Women who leave the job market during those years may find that they never catch up."[14]

Tirza Wahrman, 44, lives in Short Hills, New Jersey, and is currently at home with her children, ages 3, 8, and 10, trying to figure out the "next steps" in her career. It is an unsettling process, as Wahrman hasn't quite adjusted to her limited prospects. In the years before her children were born she had worked enormously hard to establish a blue-chip track record. She graduated from Yale Law School in 1981, worked in the antitrust division of the Justice Department, and then joined the prestigious Washington law firm of Cadwalader, Wickersham & Taft as an associate. A few years later she got married, and as she contemplated having a child, left private practice and went to work for the Port Authority in what she calls the pink-collar ghetto of public-sector law. For Wahrman it was a clear-sighted decision. She traded earning power for shorter work-weeks and generous family benefits; when her third child was born she had built up sufficient seniority to be entitled to six months of partially paid parenting leave.

Two years ago she left her Port Authority job and accompanied her husband to London, where he had a six-month assignment. On her return, she encountered serious childcare problems and as a result has spent the last year at home. She has done a little part-time work (as a court-appointed mediator), but mostly she has focused on her children.

Wahrman finds the role of "at home" mother very hard emotionally.

> I really feel the lost identity and the lowered self-esteem. And yet I know that this time with my children is very important. Just last week I was invited to speak to Deena's class about being a lawyer—the fifth grade were doing some unit on careers. Not only was I able to make time to do the talk, but I also took Deena out for a hot chocolate after class and spent an hour talking through why she felt embarrassed at having her mom speak. We ended up hitting some deep stuff. Now,

that conversation would never have happened if I
had been rushing back to my office.

But when I look into the future I'm frankly
scared about being able to resurrect a career.
Already I'm hitting an age wall. I've put out some
feelers and the law firms I've talked to aren't
interested in hiring a forty-four-year-old associate.
I feel incredibly torn. My children would benefit
from having lots of my time for a few more years,
yet if I put off reentry until my late forties, who
knows whether I will be able to find a job at
all.[15]

The real-world choices faced by Tirza Wahrman help
explain why women with children earn so much less
than women without children. Indeed, Jane Waldfogel
finds that even when you factor in differences in education and work experience, women with children earn
significantly less than women without them. In her
words, "women with children still earn about 10 percent
less per hour than women who have not had children,
even after controlling for other characteristics such as
their age, educational level, job experience, race, eth-
nicity, and so on."[16]

There is no such family penalty for men. Indeed, the
reverse is true. According to a study by Linda Waite
and Maggie Gallagher, married men with children
out-earn other men by a significant margin. Estimates

of the "family premium" for men range from 10–40 percent.[17]

Meanwhile the price women pay for their children in recent years seems to have gone up. Women without children saw their earnings rise 13 percent in the eighties and early nineties, while the earnings of women with children rose only 10 percent over the same time period. Evidence from national, time-series data reveals an especially stark picture among young women. Thirty-year-old women without children earn 90 percent of the male wage, but 30-year-old women with children earn only 73 percent of the male wage. Thus, among young women the gap between mothers and nonmothers expands to a staggering 17 percentage points.[18]

Which brings us to a central question. Who or what is to blame for this state of affairs?

Human capital theorist Solomon Polachek argues that much of the penalty attached to motherhood is caused not by employers discriminating against women with children, but by "the more implicit and subtle forms of societal discrimination taking place within the family."[19] In plain English, working women are still stuck with most family responsibilities, and this severely limits how well they can do in their careers.

Looking after a home and family continues to be hugely time-consuming. According to a recent U.K.

study, working mothers spend, on average, 62 hours a week on housework, childcare, and other sundry household duties, a figure which has risen 5 percent since the early 1990's. According to this study, mothers of preschoolers spent a total of 84 hours a week on domestic work.[20] Maternal duties may have been more strenuous in the past, but they have never been more complex than they are today. Being a responsible parent at the beginning of the twenty-first century requires the management of extensive relationships with teachers, doctors, therapists, salespeople, and assorted bureaucrats—not to mention the Internet. Sam needs a booster shot and a costume for the school play, while Samantha has just been cut from the soccer team and needs a shoulder to cry on. Meanwhile, camp applications have to be filled out, name tapes need to be sewn into the children's clothing, and an appointment has to be made with Sam's teacher to figure out why he did so badly on the most recent standardized test. And the list of things to do only becomes more complex—and harder to delegate—as children grow older.

Over the last 30 years there has been a great deal of talk about men taking on more family responsibility. And indeed, some men are doing more house-related and child-related tasks. But in the aggregate, it does not add up to much. As pointed out in chapter 2, fully 40 percent of married, high-achieving women feel that their husbands create more work for them around the house than they contribute.[21] Sad to relate, this figure does not change much between the generations. According to *High Achieving Women, 2001,* 43 percent of older women and 37 percent of younger women feel that on the home front, their husbands are a net burden.

Nora Ephron, in her 1983 book, *Heartburn,* depicted a jaundiced view of the division of household work. As she described it, in the 1970s it was fashionable to sit down with your husband and draw up a list of household duties in order to divide them equally. "This happened in thousands of households, with identical results: thousands of husbands agreed to clear the table," she wrote. "They cleared the table and then looked around as if they deserved a medal. They cleared the table and then hoped that they would never again be asked to do another thing. They cleared the table and hoped the whole thing would go away. And it mostly did."[22]

After the dust from the women's revolution had settled it turned out men's behavior had changed rather little, their contribution to routine housework had increased from a mere two to four hours a week. Wives and mothers continue to contribute the lion's share— 16 hours a week or roughly three-quarters of the total.[23] This central reality has an extremely negative impact on female earning power.

In other rich countries, the burdens of housework

and childcare are eased by government programs designed to lighten the load for working mothers: eighteen months of paid parenting leave, excellent preschools whose schedules mesh easily with the working day, and the possibility of a six-hour working day until a child is eight years old are among the best of the family-support policies offered in Europe.

According to the Harkness and Waldfogel comparative study, childbearing and child rearing seem to have a particularly depressing effect on women's wages in the United States and the United Kingdom—British women pay a penalty of 8 percent for one child and 24 percent for two children. But in the other countries covered by this study—Canada, Sweden, Australia, Germany, Finland—the "family penalty" is much lower.[24]

This study shows that significant differences among countries in the impact of children on women's wages are, in large part, the result of different family-support policies. The United States and the United Kingdom have implemented rather few family-support policies and the "family penalty" paid by United States and United Kingdom women is especially high. In fact, until the passage of the Family and Medical Leave Act (FMLA) in 1993, the United States had no national, parenting-leave policy. Even today, parenting leave American style is unpaid and excludes women who work in small companies, which means that 41 percent of working women are not entitled to any leave. With regard to childcare, although large numbers of American children are in out-of-home care, the United States relies, more heavily than other countries, on the private market to provide such care. The United Kingdom also comes up short in these areas. Unlike the United States, Britain has had paid maternity leave since 1978, but Britain's maternity leave policy is meager compared to elsewhere in Europe: it is shorter, replaces a smaller part of a woman's wage, and excludes a significant number of women . Britain also lags behind other countries in its provision of childcare. Indeed, according to a recent report by the Daycare Trust, despite a "frenetic" stream of government initiatives to improve childcare during Labour's first term in office, Britain's childcare remains the worst in Europe.[25]

Paid maternity or parenting leave seems to be particularly important to women. This is because the penalties attached to career interruptions are extremely significant. Therefore, the provision of job-protected, paid leave around childbirth, which allows women to maintain a continuous employment history through their childbearing years, has an extremely positive effect on earnings. In a study of the impact of maternity leave policies in Britain, economists Heather Joshi,

Pierella Paci, and Jane Waldfogel found that women who "quit" their jobs when they had children returned to the labor market to face considerably lower wages than mothers who took a job-protected leave and then returned to the same employer.[26]

For a century and a half American feminists have channeled much of their energy into the struggle to win formal equality with men. Early on they demanded a range of legal rights—property rights, child-custody rights, and divorce rights. Then, from the Civil War to 1920, the focus gradually narrowed to a single issue: the right to vote.

The feminist revival of the '60s and '70s brought the rights of women to the foreground once more. The National Organization for Women (NOW), formed in October 1966, revived and carried forward the nineteenth-century tradition of equal rights feminism with its stated purpose: "to take action to bring women into full participation in the mainstream of American society *now,* exercising all the privileges and responsibilities thereof in truly equal partnership."

In the beginning, NOW backed a range of goals— equal educational and job opportunities, equal pay, and access to legal abortion—but by the late 1970s its mission had narrowed to one issue: the ratification of the ERA (Equal Rights Amendment). The idea was that once all legislation that discriminated against women was gone, the playing field would be level and women could assume an equal place in society.

In Europe, various groups of social feminists have conceived the problem of the female sex quite differently. For them, it is not woman's lack of legal rights that constitute her main handicap, or even her lack of "reproductive freedom." Rather, it is her dual burden—taking care of a home and family as well as holding a job—that leads to second-class status. The goal of European social feminists has therefore been one of lightening the burden by enacting family-support policies that make this dual role less oppressive for women. The belief is that because women are wives and mothers as well as workers and citizens, they need special compensatory policies in order to accomplish as much as men in the world beyond the home. In the words of Anna Greta Leijon, a former Swedish minister of labor: "If women are to achieve equal results they need to be overcompensated in various ways." Overcompensation in Sweden has translated into an elaborate set of benefits and services for working mothers—and, increasingly, fathers.

One thing is clear: These contrasting visions of the female problem place a very different weight on motherhood. American feminists have generally stressed the ways in which women need to be treated identically to men, and have therefore sought to put aside differences. This had led them to sidetrack issues around motherhood. By and large they prefer to focus on reproductive freedom and the right to choose *not* to have a child. The critical problems around having children or being a mother are ignored or downplayed.

Social feminists, on the other hand, have placed motherhood center stage. The essence of the female problem, in their view, is to reconcile the demands of children with those of the workplace and the wider community. They believe that society at large should provide systematic support to women in recognition of their dual role as mothers and workers.

Of course, not all American feminists have been equal rights enthusiasts. In the late nineteenth century, Charlotte Perkins Gilman headed up a small band of American social feminists who identified family responsibilities as a basic cause of women's inequality. They called for a "grand domestic revolution" in women's lives and proposed kitchenless apartment houses for professional women and their families in which cleaning and cooking services would be contracted out, and children would be looked after in a shared day care and kindergarten facility. (Gilman's campaign was surely influenced by her personal experience: In 1873 she reluctantly ceded custody of her nine-year-old daughter to her ex-husband when she found that she could not both earn a living as a lecturer and be a good mother.)[27]

Fifty years later Eleanor Roosevelt was part of another group of American social feminists who pressed for protective legislation for working mothers. A forty-eight-hour workweek, the elimination of night work, and exclusion from dangerous work were key demands. Because of her belief in the importance of motherhood, Mrs. Roosevelt was a longtime opponent of the ERA. She saw equal treatment as undermining the protective laws she was fighting to put in place. Indeed, she was so irritated by the equal rights emphasis of mainstream American feminism that she refused to call herself a feminist.

The bottom line seems to be: Working mothers need more than equal treatment. Swimming in the mainstream and taking your chances doesn't produce equality of result if you're picking up 75 percent of home-related and child-related responsibilities. Equal rights *and* family supports are needed if women are to improve their earning power—and their life choices.

Despite the persuasiveness of the arguments and the data, Americans—in both the public and the private sector—remain unconvinced of the importance of such seemingly mundane matters as parenting leave, child-care and flextime.

I have bumped up against this problem at two points in my career. The first was fifteen years ago when, as executive director of the Economic Policy Council, I convened a panel of business leaders to consider how to help women bridge the family/work divide. The second was three years ago when, as part of a nationwide book tour with Cornel West, I attempted to galvanize public support for a package of family-support initiatives.

Back in 1985 I remember being extremely pleased when I succeeded in persuading the steering committee of the Economic Policy Council to establish a policy panel on work and family. Funded by the Ford and Rockefeller foundations, cochaired by Alice Illchman (then president of Sarah Lawrence College), and John Sweeney (then president of the EIU), the new panel was impressive. Its members included Gerald Ford (former president), Kay Graham (the late chairman of the Washington Post Company), Steve Ross (the late chairman of Warner Bros.) and Henry Kaufman (then chief economist at Salomon Brothers). I was thrilled. Just the sort of luminaries to prod the private sector into action, I thought. However, when the time came to convene the panel and put these illustrious people to work, I got a rude awakening. Most of my distinguished male members simply failed to turn up. When I met with them and attempted to explain why they should take this project seriously, they either yawned or raised their eyebrows.

After listening to my pitch, Henry Kaufman looked embarrassed and told me rather lamely that he was not "up to speed" in this policy area. Couldn't he, he asked me, join one of our other panels? I should point out that this man was not a shrinking violet. In general, he had no problem speaking out on subjects as diverse as Japanese defense policy, immigration reform and Third World debt—not all areas where he would be considered an expert. Yet somehow, issues like maternity leave and childcare seemed to make him very nervous. But it was not just nerves. I could have dealt with an attack of nerves. When pushed, Kaufman revealed another reason behind his reluctance to get involved: family supports smacked of government interference. He was all for equal rights for women, but he was not sure he liked the notion of government meddling in private lives or telling companies what to do.

The female reaction was even more difficult to take. Most of the distinguished female panel members weren't interested either. Marina Whitman, a senior vice president at GM and former member of the Council of Economic Advisors, excused herself on the grounds that she could not afford to become, as she put it "contaminated" by this panel. As she explained, "It has taken me fifteen years to get a hard-nosed reputation, and I just daren't risk it. If I were to get involved in these messy women's issues, it could do me a lot of harm in the company." A kind woman, she followed this up with a piece of personal advice: "If I were you I would drop this whole project. You're a woman who has had enough sense to build a career in a serious field. Why risk diluting your reputation?"

Another woman panel member, Katherine Graham, threatened to resign because I would not take childcare off the agenda. We had always planned to spend at least two panel sessions on this critical problem, so I was amazed when Graham called, just before the first childcare meeting, and tried to derail it. "I don't know what childcare has to do with the employment problems of women," she said militantly. "If a woman chooses to have children she should deal with the consequences." I opened my mouth, intending to explain how children were a societal as well as an individual responsibility. But then I closed it again. I didn't know how to deal with such entrenched hostility.

The project limped along for two years and eventually produced a report that seemed, at least on the surface, to be pretty important. I mean, how many times has a private-sector group signed off on a cluster of family-support initiatives that include paid, parenting leave, flextime, and subsidized childcare! But it was hard to get excited. I knew the inside story and understood that without the personal commitment of my illustrious panel members none of the recommendations contained in the report would result in action.

After the panel disbanded, I spent quite a long time pondering why these well-meaning men and women had failed to warm to the task at hand. As far as the men were concerned, I concluded that many of them had been molded by the fifties and at some level believed that children should be looked after by their mothers; corporations and government should not make it easy for women to shirk their responsibilities. These attitudes neatly complemented their preference for free markets. These were the Reagan years, after all, and government was increasingly seen as inept or irrelevant. Particularly when it came to private lives, the general feeling was that the less government interference, the better.

And as for the women, they had a different set of issues. Ideologically, they were resistant to the idea that working mothers might need special supports or benefits. They had absorbed the message of equal rights feminism and were convinced that women had a better shot at equality if they behaved exactly like men. In the words of one panel member: "If women want power, money, and status in the wider world, nothing is more effective than 'cloning the male competitive model.'"

A subset of these women also had personal reasons for being unenthusiastic about family benefits. They themselves were childless, and mixed in with their policy perspective was a heavy dose of disappointment and resentment. They had a hard time empathizing with younger women who, in the eyes of at least one panel member, "have no business feeling entitled to both a career and children."

Twelve years after my experience with the Economic Policy Council, on a nationwide book tour, I became reacquainted with the difficulty of "selling" a program of family supports. In 1998 Cornel West and I wrote *The War Against Parents,* a book based on several years of research, describing the forces pitted against parents these days. In it we detailed how adults raising children have been hurt by this country's economic policies and popular culture, and we devoted a large section to solutions. The final two chapters included a *Parents' Bill of Rights*—our response to the urgent needs of moms and dads around the nation.

Given the several years of research that had gone into this book we had a fair idea of the range and scope of the onslaught on parents. What we hadn't anticipated was the virulence of the attack. In the summer of 1998 we spent six weeks on the road speaking in eight states and 28 communities, and found that while our book had taken an accurate measure of the forces ranged against moms and dads, it had failed to appreciate the emotional intensity of the battle in which parents are engaged.

In some states and cities parent bashers seemed to own the airwaves. On talk radio shows such as the John and Ken Morning Show (KABC radio in Los Angeles) and the Geoff Metcalf Show (KSFO radio in San Francisco), callers were often semicoherent, so white-hot was their rage. By their reports, neighborhoods in California are packed to the gills with welfare queens and self-absorbed professionals raising out-of-control kids on taxpayers' dollars.

And then, in public libraries, churches, and community centers we met group after group of demoralized parents. From the Allen Temple Baptist Church in Oakland, California, to the New York Public Library in Manhattan, parents felt hurt—trapped in a lonely, thankless struggle, beaten back by a tidal wave of blame. In Chicago, one father of three summed up the feelings of many: "Parents somehow have become the fall guys, taking the rap for the consequences of America's careless, unbridled individualism."

Looking back on that book tour, we probably caught the first stirrings of what is now a full-fledged backlash against parents and children. Starting early last year, adults without children—they call themselves "child-free"—began to organize, accusing parents of grabbing more than their fair share of public dollars, of "wanting a child and a Lexus, too." In her book *The Baby Boon,* which appeared in early 2000, journalist Elinor Burkett makes the extraordinary claim that the "past decade has seen the most massive redistribution of wealth since the War on Poverty—this time not from rich to poor, but from nonparents to parents." She sees herself as spearheading a "simmering backlash against perks for parents."

Burkett is moderate compared to many of her child-free peers. Some of the more extreme can be found in cyberspace where there has been a proliferation of websites with names like "I'd Rather Talk to My Toaster" and "Unruly, Ill-Mannered Yard Apes." These sites walk you through a litany of complaints about parents ("Breeders feel entitled to take constant time off for child-related issues whereby their coworkers become burdened with additional workloads"; "Breeders seek fertility treatments and give birth to a frankenspawn litter") and refer to children as "anklebiters," "crib lizards," "crotch fruit," "fartlings," "germ mongers," and "spawn."

If these attacks had not become seriously ugly it would be easier to reach out with empathy and understanding to members of this new childfree movement. They do after all have a point. Some of America's biggest and best-run companies have developed elaborate programs of family support. In a world where most workers feel newly pushed and squeezed, it must be exceedingly tantalizing to find some of the best company policies "off-limits" because you don't happen to have a child.

While conceding this point, I would like to emphasize a larger perspective. The reality is, American parents actually enjoy rather few perks or benefits. Fewer than half of even large companies offer substantial family supports, and this figure plummets for small companies. What is more, over the last 30 years government policy has tilted *against* rather than in favor of parents. According to economist Edward Wolff, the relative well-being of parents compared to childless adults has been continuously eroded over the past 40 years "with government policy being the powerful driving force."[28] The fact is, we as a country have hugely expanded the benefits for families without children (social security and medicaid are good examples), while cutting back on benefits for families with children. Tax reductions for dependent children have been vastly reduced, while welfare programs that provide benefits to poor families have been substantially reduced and time limits introduced.[29] The rather few family-support policies that exist are noteworthy for their mean-spirit-edness. Parenting leave, for example, is unpaid and excludes those who work for small companies.

Elinor Burkett and her childfree peers are much more wrong than right. Yes, there has been a redistri-bution of wealth in this society, but it has gone from parents to nonparents, not the other way around.

In the year 2002 we seem to have an impressive array of forces lined up against working women: tra-ditional men who don't like women shirking their domestic responsibilities and are antagonistic to gov-ernment interference in private lives; equal rights fem-inists, who continue to downplay the importance of family benefits; and a new mini-movement of the child-free who, oddly enough, are convinced that parents already get way too much in terms of perks and privileges.

Given this environment, can businesses and gov-ernment be expected to launch any new initiatives to help women balance their lives? This question will dominate chapters 6 and 7.

One final note. In a wide-ranging interview in the spring of 2000, Harvard Law School professor Mary Ann Glendon reflected on the long-term consequences of so many high-achieving women living out their lives without having children. In her words, "We are in uncharted territory here: for the first time in history large numbers of women occupy leadership positions and almost half of these new female leaders—unlike male leaders—are childless. Will this affect our goals and values? Will it affect our programmatic agenda? You bet it will. People without children have a much weaker stake in our collective future. As our leadership group tilts toward childlessness, we can expect it to become even harder to pay for our schooling system or for measures that might prevent global warming. America's rampant individualism is about to get a whole lot worse."[30]

4

PREDATORS AND
NURTURERS

High-achieving Women and the Shortage of Men

O N A B A L M Y E V E N I N G I N E A R L Y
September, the penthouse suite of Lifeworks on lower
Fifth Avenue was filling with women, who had come
to hear psychologist Marilyn Graman, president and
founder of Lifeworks, describe the workshop and seminars offered by her organization. There were about 60
women in all, most of them expensively dressed, brief-
case-toting professionals. The majority seemed to be in
their forties, but there was a smattering of younger
and older women—a stunning African-American
woman in her twenties, and a faded beauty in her sixties caught my eye because they were both wearing
leopard skin boots.

A few of them knew each other—they had obviously met at other Lifeworks seminars—but most did not. They pinned on name tags (first names only), collected their bottled water, and eyed each other warily. A small group of us exchanged polite chitchat as we found our chairs and waited for the event to begin.

I sat down next to Carolyn, a dark-haired woman in an elegant Armani suit, who introduced herself and seemed eager to talk. She told me she had read about Lifeworks in *The New York Times* the week she turned 40 and decided to check it out. She felt she had a firm grip on the career thing but needed some heavy-duty help on the dating front. She had worked as a lawyer on Wall Street for the last ten years and her job had pretty much "obliterated" her private life.

Then Graman—a statuesque woman wearing a black caftan—swept into the room and quickly got down to business. It was a one-two punch. First, she caught the attention of this sophisticated group by sharing a few tantalizing insights: "There are plenty of men in New York City and at least one juicy one who wants to marry you. But to find this man you need to get rid of the armor you have built up over the years. Think about it," Graman said, leaning over her microphone and lowering her voice. "Any attractive woman who is single at age forty has been dating for twenty-five years and has a long and complicated history of hurting and being hurt. You may not know it, but you've developed a thick suit of protective armor that makes you cold and unapproachable. I can show you how to break through this armor and become much more alluring and nurturing." Inside the room you could hear a pin drop.

Graman then changed gear and walked briskly through the Lifeworks offerings. For women who were time-pressed she flagged two short courses, each of which met for a long weekend: "Having What You Want with a Man" and "The Natural Power of Being a Woman." For those who were urgent in their desire to get married she recommended "Marriage Works," a six-month, 276-hour course intended to lead a woman directly to the altar. The cost: a cool $9,600. Graman described "Marriage Works" as "particularly appropriate for 40–50-year-old women with loudly ticking biological clocks; it could be the only way of finding a husband quickly enough to get a child in under the wire.

As Graman described it, "Marriage Works" is part group therapy and part personal pep talk. It's organized into various sections, each of which deals with a different aspect of the mating game: 40 hours are devoted to studying why participants might have a "relationship block"; 26 hours are allocated to talking with a "guide," a coach-cum-cheerleader who has already reaped the fruits of a Graman course; and 11 hours are spent discussing decor and ambiance (participants are encouraged to paint the walls of their apartments in soft, sexy colors and banish exercise equipment from their bedrooms). Participants also spend nine hours learning how to move gracefully and eight hours on clothes selection (buttoned-up jackets and pinstripes are strongly discouraged). A final three and a half hours are spent on the art of gracious gift receiving. According to Graman, executive women have no idea of how to accept a gift gracefully.

"Marriage Works" finishes with a field trip to a bridal shop where the women try on white, tulle dresses, experiment with blue garters, and visualize their wedding day. "If you see it, you can have it," says Graman with deep conviction.

During the break, I talked to Maureen Walsh, business director of Lifeworks. Walsh, a fast-talking MBA type who used to be marketing director for the Brooklyn Academy of Music, filled me in on the clientele and didn't pull punches: "A typical participant in one of our courses is a business executive who forgot to make time for a personal life," she says. "And between you and me, these are very prickly women. They've been wearing pants too long. Men like powerful women, but they don't want to be eaten alive. Believe me, I've been there and I know."

After the seminar, my new friend Carolyn shared a cab uptown with me. She was all fired up for "Marriage Works" and couldn't stop talking about what she'd learned. "When Marilyn Graman talked about twenty-five years of failed dates and the development of protective armor, it was as though a light-bulb lit up in my head. I thought, Oh my God, that's me! I don't mean to, but maybe I do come across as some kind of cold-blooded predator." I dropped Carolyn off outside her building on East 73rd Street, and as she stepped out of the cab she threw me a parting question: "What do you think? Is this suit a little too buttoned-up and masculine? Should I try something more feminine?"[1]

For those of us who came of age in the bracing climate of equal rights feminism, it is extremely difficult to take something like Lifeworks seriously. I remember so clearly singing "Free to Be You and Me" to my daughter Lisa when she was three years old and telling her the story of Atalanta, a girl athlete so strong and brave that she ran faster than anyone else in the land. Was I now supposed to tell 23-year-old Lisa that it's possible to be *too* strong and *too* brave? That a grown-up Atalanta would have a hard time on the dating front and would need a Marilyn Graman to teach her how to land a man?

But I don't mean to be supercilious, it's all too easy

to make fun of experts like Marilyn Graman and courses like Lifeworks. The fact is, anxiety about finding a mate has become a huge issue in our culture. Best-selling books, afternoon talk shows, and women's magazines are filled with heavy-duty, heavy-handed advice on how to find a husband.

A few months ago I walked into the Harvard Co-op and found, in the relationship section, 62 books on the mating game. Three were directed at men, 11 were written for both men and women, and 48 targeted women exclusively. Three entire shelves of books were devoted to teaching women how to flatter, tease, dupe, and otherwise manipulate a man into marriage. Titles included: *How to Give Your Single Love Life a Himplant; What Makes a Man Cross the Line from Like to Love: Get a Life, Then Get a Man; What Men Want: Three Professional Single Men Reveal to Women What It Takes to Make a Man Yours; Getting to "I Do"*; and, *The Rules: Time-Tested Secrets for Capturing the Heart of Mr. Right*. To give a sense of the reach of these books, *The Rules* has sold more than two million copies nationwide and has spawned a cottage industry of Wannabe Rules.

Of course, hip, high-achieving, Harvard women are often embarrassed to show an interest in books with titles like *Getting to "I Do."* The day I was in the Co-op

I noticed a well-put-together woman—somewhere in her thirties—skimming through some books in the relationship section. My presence obviously made her uncomfortable. She started fidgeting and shifting from foot to foot, then moved to a neighboring section, put the books she had been reading on an empty shelf, covered them with some papers, and walked out of the store. I looked at the titles when she was gone. They were *The Rules;* and *What Men Want.* She'd covered them with a class handout—an MBA case study.

The appetite for advice on how to find a man is enormous—and, of course, not limited to America. *Bridget Jones's Diary,* a novel by Helen Fielding chronicling a London woman's search for Mr. Right, became a runaway best-seller worldwide in 1996.[2] To date it has sold almost five million copies and spawned a best-selling sequel, *Bridget Jones: The Edge of Reason,* as well as a hugely successful feature film starring Renee Zellweger, Hugh Grant, and Colin Firth.

Self-mocking and seriously funny, Bridget Jones describes herself as "a desperate re-tread with a sell-by date" in a world where all the men want someone younger. In all kinds of ways she is an unlikely heroine. Yes, she's edgy and modern. With closet drawers crammed with "a fury of black opaque panty hose twisted into ropelike tangles," and a matter-of-fact attitude toward "shagging," she comes across as an endearing version of the sexy career women featured in television shows like *Sex and the City*. But she's also extraordinarily dated. The nakedness of her search for Mr. Right is worthy of Jane Austen. Indeed, it is right out of Jane Austen. It's no coincidence that Bridget's love interest is called Mr. Darcy (who stands around looking snooty in much the same way his forbear did in *Pride and Prejudice*), and parts of the story line are taken directly from *Persuasion*. As far as the urgency women feel to find Mr. Right goes, not much has changed over the last two centuries.

Books like *The Rules* and *Bridget Jones's Diary* may be hard to swallow—and for progressive women with feminist instincts, they are particularly hard to swallow—but the truth is, much of the new anxiety is grounded in reality. Thirty-something career women seeking to find a suitable mate face tremendous challenges that range from timing difficulties to deep-seated attitudinal problems. Let's start with the issue of timing.

Increasingly, delaying marriage and children seems like the sensible thing to do. As we saw in chapter 3, large numbers of ambitious, accomplished women seek to postpone family until they have their graduate degrees in hand and their careers securely under way. The problem is, careers these days are not quickly or easily launched. If you are a business executive, lawyer, or banker with a "high-altitude career," you may well be working 60 hours a week deep into your thirties, and by this time the marriage market has turned against you. Simply put: The younger a woman is, the more men she has to choose from.

Remember that famous 1986 study—by Yale sociologist Neil Bennett and Harvard economist David Bloom—which purported to find that a forty-year-old woman had a better chance of being shot by terrorists than getting married for the first time?[3] According to Bennett and Bloom, at age 30 a never-married college-educated woman had a 20 percent chance of getting married, but by 40 her chances had dropped to 1.3 percent. This study hit such a nerve that it was picked up by the wire services and featured in newspapers and on news shows across the world before it was even formally published. Bennett told me he spent weeks fielding phone calls from journalists in countries as far afield as Australia and Argentina.[4]

The Bennett and Bloom data stirred up a furious debate—and inspired a slew of new studies. When the dust settled, it turned out that although the odds were not nearly as dismal as first advertised, Bennett and Bloom were quite correct in their conclusion: the older she gets, the harder it is for a college-educated woman to find a husband.

The contemporary figures are persuasive. According to *High-Achieving Women, 2001,* marriage rates tail off quite dramatically as women get older. Only 10 percent of high-achieving women in this survey got married for the first time after age 30, and only 1 percent after age 35. Recent demographic data help explain why.[5] At age 28 there are four eligible men for every three college-educated, single women. At age 38, however, there is only one eligible man for every three college-educated, single women.

These Census Bureau data—which simply match single women with slightly older single men who have a similar or higher level education—actually overstates the likelihood that an older, college-educated woman will find a husband. In reality, highly educated, high-earning men seeking a wife don't limit themselves to high-achieving women in their own age bracket, but instead reach into a larger pool that includes younger women who do not necessarily match these men in either education or achievement. This pool of women only expands as men get older. For women, the opposite is true. College-educated women tend to seek husbands who are slightly older and have even higher levels of education and achievement than they do. This relatively limited pool tends to get smaller as women age.

In other words, as time rolls on, a high-achieving

woman looking for a suitable mate finds herself running into fierce competition—not only with other accomplished women in her own age bracket, but also with large numbers of younger, less-accomplished women who have much to offer high-achieving men. And what they have to offer may have nothing to do with education or earning power—or sex or beauty for that matter. Admiration and attention are two qualities that spring to mind. A less-accomplished twenty-something is not necessarily sexier or more beautiful than an extremely accomplished thirty-something, but she may well be more willing to pay attention to a high-earning man and be more impressed by his accomplishments. When Tamara Adler talked about how men in high-altitude careers crave women who can pony up the "wow" factor, she was essentially talking about the competitive advantage of younger, less-accomplished and more-easily-impressed women.

All of which leads to my second point: that timing difficulties are made much more complicated—and harder to deal with—by complex attitudinal problems.

Karen Maguire, 28, the young associate at Paine-Webber we met in chapter 3, had an extremely clear-eyed understanding of male attitudes toward marriage. She referred me to *Bobos in Paradise*—a recent book by journalist David Brooks. What caught her eye was

Brooks's take on predators and nurturers and how they pair up in the marriage market. In her view, Brooks hit the nail on the head.

"When I read this book, I just had this flash of recognition. I mean most of the people I work with are classic predators. If you're not aggressive and tough when you start out, you surely end up that way. This is the kind of job that turns you into a predator. It's how you succeed in this business.

"How does this factor into relationships and marriage? This is something I think about a lot."

In his book, Brooks describes modern-day predators as the lawyers, traders, and bankers who spend their lives negotiating over or competing for money and power and are comfortable "being tough and screwing others."[6] Nurturers, on the other hand, have a different mind-set. They are academics, policy wonks, journalists, and artists—people who deal with ideas or spend their time helping others, cooperating with others, or facilitating something. They tend to be much more supportive and empathetic. Brooks examines the wedding pages of *The New York Times,* and in a not very systematic piece of analysis, tries to ascertain whether predators are marrying fellow predators or whether predators are marrying nurturers. He finds that it is fairly evenly split.

Karen is skeptical about Brooks's results:

They don't ring true to me. Or at least, they're only part of the story. Why on earth would a male predator seek out a female predator as a potential mate? I mean, what would they then do: eat each other for dinner? I tell you, predator guys are turned on by us. We're exciting and we've got lots of status these days. Let's face it, it's a feather in your cap if you can squire around a woman who has an MBA from Wharton. But you won't want to marry this woman unless she's prepared to curb her ambition and give you pride of place.

I know this guy who's a standard predator type. He's just finishing up at Harvard Business School and is about to move to Austin, Texas, where he has a job with a venture capital firm. Well, last year he broke up with a long-standing girlfriend, just came right out and told her he didn't want to marry her because he wasn't ready to commit.

The break-up caused her to become much more ambitious. I guess she decided that if she couldn't have the marriage thing she might as well go for the career thing. So she applied to Harvard Business School and got in. Well, this friend of mine, her ex-boyfriend got wind of this and it piqued his interest—it's as though success made her desirable again. So he took her out to a fancy restaurant and told her that he would marry her after all as long as she turned down Harvard

Business School and moved to Austin to be with him. And guess what. She said yes!"

And so they're getting married. And for the rest of his life my friend will be telling the story of how his wife turned down Harvard Business School to marry him.

I find it all very disheartening. Guys like you to do well—get into the best graduate school, land the prestigious job—it increases your value and reflects well on them. But they then want you to give it all up because they don't really want you to focus on the big career; they want you to focus on them.

Brooks thinks he found examples of predators marrying predators, but I bet my bottom dollar that his male predators turned the female predators into nurturers overnight. They just can't stand the competition.

A little later in our conversation, I asked Karen why she felt so strongly about Brooks's take on predators and nurturers.

Karen laughed.

It's personal! Of course it's personal. Remember my telling you about last night? I got together with some guy friends—really close friends that I have known since college. Well, during the course of the evening I realized that here I was talking to three really successful, attractive men—you would

call them eligible men—who weren't remotely
interested in me as a potential mate. Now that
they have real jobs and are looking around for
someone who might be wife material, they are dating women who are younger than I am and much
less ambitious. I mean, I am not even in the running. I kidded them about their taste in women,
but in reality I felt rejected. I guess I got excited
about predators and nurturers because these
labels made their choices seem a little less hurtful.[7]

And the voice of this honest, gutsy woman tailed off.

As I pointed out to Karen, there are a slew of psychological theories that underscore the predator/nur-
turer split and support her perspective on marriage.
According to Judith Wallerstein, founder of the
California-based Center for the Family in Transition
and author of several books on marriage and divorce:

When it comes to marriage, the notion of comple-
mentarity is extremely important. Individuals
often seek out a mate who brings something
entirely different to the table. It strikes me as
highly probable that a hard-driving, high-earning
man would not want a replica of himself, but
would be attracted to a woman who has an
entirely different bundle of attributes. She might,
for example, know about beautiful things, or she
might *be* a beautiful thing!

It's also true that many successful men want to come home after a hard day in the office to a wife who says, "Poor dear. Did you have a hard day? Have a martini." The problem with casting a peer in the wifely role is that even if she is able to conjure up the time and actually be there to greet him when he gets home, it is much more difficult for her to be simply comforting. Her words might have an edge to them. She might well ask a bunch of probing, critical questions, and dish out some advice. This is not what he is looking for.[8]

Thoroughly intrigued by Wallerstein's viewpoint, I decided to talk with some men. This turned out to be easier said than done. High-achieving predator types were difficult to pin down. It's not so much that these men didn't want to talk, it's more that they didn't want to take the time. With eyes firmly focused on the bottom line, they saw no obvious "upside" in talking to me.

After casting around for a few weeks I came up with a candidate. My stepdaughter's boyfriend called in a favor—a buddy from business school—and hours later, Joe Schmidt, a 31-year-old project manager at Goldman Sachs, called me to say he would be delighted to give me his take on women and marriage.

Schmidt and I met at an Upper West Side tapas bar on a particularly cold January evening. On the phone he had described himself as "kind of short and balding" so I was surprised when this good-looking, smiley guy walked over and introduced himself. Warm and charming, he put both of us at ease. After ordering drinks I asked him whether he knew any female predators.

His eyes lit up with instant recognition.

There's a whole bunch of them where I work. They're armed to the teeth with degrees—MBAs and the like—they're real aggressive, they love to take control, and they have this fierce hunger for success and for stuff. Everything they do and everything they want is expensive. Taking one of these women out for a beer after work can mean blowing a hundred bucks on a round of drinks at Whisky Blue.

The thing is, you can't spend your way to happiness. Sure, you can work hard and buy lots of stuff, because there's no limit to the amount of stuff in the world, so you end up on a treadmill. When I look for a woman, I'm not looking for someone who will exaggerate this craziness.

So I take it you wouldn't want to marry one of these women?" I searched his face for confirmation, but Schmidt looked a little troubled.

I didn't mean to sound off about money. Some of these women are a kick—they dress well, look good, and have a kind of authority and stature.

You've got to be pretty impressive to survive as a woman in the financial world. I didn't mean to put them down. But there are some pretty solid reasons why I wouldn't want to marry one of them.

First off, I look around at my friends, and I tell you, when a high-flying man marries a high-flying woman the strain is intense, especially if they have children. They're both trying to conquer the world and they're both under huge pressure. They end up with no time for one another. It's just much too difficult. I don't want to end up having to make a date with my wife if I want to see her.

It's also true that I don't have much to offer one of these women. They have everything already. I mean, I want my success in the world and my earning power to matter—and to be appreciated.

One final thing, and this is important. I'm money-driven enough and would want my wife to bring something different to the relationship—tenderness, expressiveness, even a little silliness. I need someone who will help me wind down and smell the roses. I guess I think marriage is about creating a life, not building a bank account.

Schmidt sipped his drink and then added, rather sheepishly,

I dream of a woman with a wonderful smile and expressive eyes. I see her as dedicated and hard-

working, but not driven or grasping; definitely a
nurturing type. Ideally, I would like her to be
involved in work she cares about but this work
should not dominate her life. And a fierce commitment to skiing or white-water rafting wouldn't
hurt.

He smiled, acknowledging the humor in having such a
laundry list of demands.

"But," I prodded gently, "you haven't said anything
about education, earnings, or professional achievement."

Schmidt laughed. "I guess that gives it away—those
kinds of things are way down the list for me."

Schmidt grew up on Long Island. His dad was a
truck farmer who made a good living growing let-
tuces, potatoes, tomatoes, and pumpkins. Schmidt
attended Manhattan College, worked for a few years,
then returned to school, earning an MBA at NYU. He
then took a job at Goldman Sachs, managing the communications and data processing operations of this
giant investment bank—sophisticated systems that are
constantly in need of fine-tuning and upgrading. "My
job has its downside," says Schmidt.

I work a six-day week—over sixty hours—and
don't get paid that much. This year I'll earn about
$200,000, which isn't high by the standards of

Wall Street. But I like my work. I'm a restless, practical sort of person and this kind of trouble-shooting suits me.

I asked him what he wanted his life to look like at age 45. "That's easy. I want the whole storybook deal. A wife, three kids, a nice house, a couple of cars in the driveway, and some land. I guess it's the farmer in me, but I really would like some land."

"And how about your wife?" I asked. "Will she be at home with the kids or working?"

Schmidt paused and picked his words carefully.

I want to say, "whatever floats her boat" because I want her to be happy. But deep down, I hope she chooses to be home with the kids, at least for a few years. The thing is, I want the woman I marry— the woman I love—to be the one instilling values in our kids. I want to come home at night and have her tell me all the neat stuff the kids have done and said that day. My mom was home when I was growing up, and I remember that as being incredibly important. I could call home any hour of the day and she would be there ready to do whatever.

I had one last question for him. "What if marriage doesn't work out for you and you ended up not having children? Would this be a big deal for you?"

He shot back an answer, as quick as lightning. "It would be a disaster, a total disaster."

> Having a wife and kids is huge for me. My grand-father was one of eighteen and my father was one of five. I mean, this is what life is all about. If someone gave me the choice between 10 million dollars or a couple of kids, it would be a no-brainer. Of course I'd take the kids. So I better not get too picky because it's getting to be urgent—this business of finding a wife.
>
> There's all this talk about women's biological clocks, but I have a clock, too. I mean, if I want three kids and want to finish up on the kid front by the time I'm forty-two, I need to get married real soon—and I'm working on it.

And Schmidt gave me a wide grin. Earlier in the evening he had hinted that there was a pretty special 26-year-old in his life, but this relationship had been off-limits in our conversation.

"Why forty-two?" I asked. "It seems very precise."

"Well, my dad died from a heart attack when he was fifty-eight. Now he smoked for forty years and I'm a nonsmoker, so probably I'm not at risk in the same way, but it kind of hangs over me. Getting my kids through childhood before I hit sixty is important to me."[9]

Looking back on our conversation, Joe Schmidt does not strike me as a typical predator. He is much too empathetic to fit the typology laid out in *Bobos in Paradise*. But despite Schmidt's lack of predatory edge, his attitudes about women and marriage spell trouble for high-achieving women like Karen Maguire. Schmidt is simply seeking a different kind of woman. The attributes that help define Maguire's core identity—education, ambition, earning power—are not among those he necessarily wants in a wife.

But male attitudes are only part of the challenge facing ambitious women today. Women bring their own very complicated issues to relationships, not least of which is an extremely skeptical view of marriage itself. The attitudes of Anne Kimball, 26, and Vicki Townsend, 27, are relatively common among women in their mid- to late-twenties.

We met at Starbucks in Cambridge, Massachusetts, one blustery Tuesday in October 2000. Anne (the daughter of a close friend of mine) had chosen the venue because it was close to her place of work. She had just completed her MBA and had a brand-new job at a high-tech company with a boss who kept her on a tight rein, so she felt constrained to keep her lunch break short. Vicki, Anne's best friend from high school and a grad student at BU, had taken the T in from Boston.

Anne and Vicki already knew what I wanted to talk about—we had spoken by phone—so as soon as we were settled with our sandwiches I delved in: "Anne," I said, "do you want to get married?"

Her response was quick. "Everyone I know who got married eventually got divorced. Why should I want to get divorced?" As Anne explained it, her hostile knee-jerk reaction has a lot to do with what she went through as a child. Her parents split when she was nine years old, and as she put it, "my parents' divorce seemed to trigger a bunch of other divorces. Over the next five years the parents of seven of my friends split up. I felt as though an earthquake had moved through my community leaving a huge amount of wreckage. The tearing and the wrenching were pretty bad. For a few years in there most of us kids had these crazed parents—acting out, freaking out, never available.

"I now feel like some kind of poster child for the long-term effects of divorce. People talk about the 'sleeper effects' of divorce." Anne gave a forced, hard laugh. "Well, it turns out I have most of them. I have a hard time trusting men and an even harder time making a commitment. I guess it will be another ten years before I can even think about marriage."

At that point Vicki chipped in, "I feel the same way, but for different reasons. I'm not dealing with the fallout of divorce—my parents are still together—but I'm a long way from being 'ready' for marriage. Here I am back in grad school, not knowing what I want to do when I grow up. Maybe I'll settle down and teach, but maybe I'll surprise myself and go join the Peace Corps for two years. I've always wanted to spend a chunk of time in Africa. In so many ways my life is still up for grabs. I'm 27, but I'm still a kid."[10]

In an arm's length, abstract kind of way, most young women want to get married. According to a 2001 survey, 83 percent of college women agree with the statement that "being married is a very important goal for me."[11] But at least for high-achieving women, this bedrock aspiration is overlain with a thick layer of distrust and skepticism, which seriously gets in the way.

According to Bonnie Maslin, a New York–based psychologist who has written extensively on marriage:

> Women in their twenties are searching for emotional connection, self-fulfillment, and happiness, not marriage per se. Indeed, the women I see in my practice have a rather "degraded" view of marriage as an institution. They tend to view it as irrelevant, risky, or just way out there in the future.
>
> Why is this so? Part of the reason is that we live in a culture that is immensely narcissistic, and young people—men and women—are enamored

of the freedom that goes along with being single. They see marriage as something that will hem them in and limit their range of choice.

Part of the reason is that accomplished women are doing very nicely on their own. They fear the risk of divorce and they don't actually need the security of a Mrs. degree. Women no longer have to get married to attain a comfortable middle-class lifestyle, and there's no particular stigma attached to remaining single.

And part of the reason is that women these days prefer to put marriage on hold until they have forged an authentic identity. But growing a career—and various types of inner strength and coherence—are endeavors that can take a decade or two.[12]

Maslin's bottom line? "Today's thirty-eight-year-old woman is yesterday's twenty-eight-year-old in terms of readiness for marriage. These days, a serious interest in marriage is often triggered by the desire to have a child before it's too late. Very few women actually want to go the turkey-baster route. So some time in their thirties women are ready to settle—to pay what they consider to be the price in terms of lost opportunity and autonomy."

The problem is, a 38-year-old woman (or even a 35-year-old) may well have missed the boat. As we understand from the demographic data, by this point in time the marriage market has turned against her and infertility has begun to rear its ugly head.

But women don't seem to understand these facts fully—or at least they don't understand them early enough. My interviews with women in their twenties revealed a great deal of skittishness about marriage, but very little sense of urgency. Karen Maguire is highly unusual. Her elaborate backward-mapping exercises are more typical of the 35-year-olds I met than of the 28-year-olds.

But let's take a closer look at the roots of women's skepticism about marriage.

Over the last 30 years the idea that marriage is good for men and bad for women has become an established fact for educated American women. Back in the early seventies, sociologist Jessie Bernard planted the seed for this now widely accepted notion in her acclaimed book, *The Future of Marriage*. In it, she argued that "in every marital union there are really two marriages, his and hers," and his is a whole lot better than hers.[13] For husbands, marriage brings health and happiness; for wives, marriage brings depression and lower self-esteem. According to Bernard, marriage affects women like a low-grade fever, gradually debilitating her emotional and mental state. Indeed, Bernard believed that marriage was so fundamentally bad for women that any housewife claiming to be happy must be out of her mind. In her words, "we do not clip wings or bind feet, but we do . . . 'deform' the minds of girls, as traditional Chinese used to deform their feet, in order to shape them for happiness in marriage."[14]

Her study fell on fertile ground. In the early 1970s, cultural attitudes were changing and people were prepared to believe that marriage threatened an individual's ability to realize his or her capabilities. An emerging human potential movement contended that autonomy, growth, and creativity were the highest forms of human development and marriage was something that interfered. At the same time, new-wave feminists were beginning to stress ways in which the patriarchal institution of marriage severely limited a woman's ability to pursue any type of self-development. Radical feminists talked about the ways in which marriage constituted "slavery" and "legalized rape," while more mainstream types talked about the ways in which marriage circumscribed a woman's intellectual horizons and caused her to suppress her sense of self.

There was more than a grain of truth in these attacks on marriage. As Betty Friedan described so convincingly in *The Feminine Mystique,* marriage, fifties-style, could be suffocating, particularly for college-educated women. They had a hard time seeing how "clearing up after three meals a day, getting at the

fuzz behind the radiators with the hard rubber appli-
ance of the vacuum cleaner, emptying wastebaskets,
and washing bathroom floors day after day, week after
week, year after year, added up to a sum total of anything except minutiae that, laid end to end, reach
nowhere."[15] After a steady diet of housework that
could be "capably handled by an eight-year-old"[16]—to
use Friedan's words—these women were ready to
leave the doll's house and spark a women's revolution.

Forty years have now rolled by and women have
won a great many new freedoms both inside and outside the home. For today's young women, the relevant
question is: what does marriage 2001-style do to a
woman's life? Does it help her achieve health, wealth,
and happiness? Or does it trigger depression and
expose her to other serious risks? Over the last ten
years research has been trickling out to suggest either
that Bernard's pessimism was unfounded, or that marriage is actually becoming healthier for women.[17]

Let's start with mental health. Thirty years ago
Bernard contended that marriage caused women to be
unhappy and depressed. Recent research shows quite
the opposite. A 1996 Rutgers University study that
followed the mental health of 1,400 young men and
women over a seven-year period found that marriage
boosted the happiness or well-being of both sexes and
that young adults who got and stayed married had

higher levels of well-being than those who remained single.[18] Similarly, a recent study by David Blanchflower and Andrew Oswald, which examined life satisfaction among 100,000 randomly sampled Americans and Britons from the early 1970s to the 1990s, found that the well-being of women fell over this time period mainly due to a fall-off in the number of women who were married. In both countries, this twenty-year time span saw a large increase in the number of women who either never married, or divorced.[19]

Money, health, and sex are also areas where the new research is unequivocal: women are better off when married. Blanchflower and Oswald demonstrate that in both the United States and Britain, a lasting marriage is worth approximately $100,000 over a lifetime when compared to being widowed or divorced. While Linda Waite and Maggie Gallagher, in their book *The Case for Marriage,* show that while the marriage premium is particularly high for men, it is also significant for women. Married men seem to make better workers than single men: they have lower rates of absenteeism and work longer hours. As a result married men earn somewhere between 10 percent and 40 percent more than single men. For women, the relationship between marriage and money is more complicated. Married women without children receive a small marriage premium, ranging from 5 percent to 10 percent, but the big boost for married women comes in the form of security in old age. Married couples save a good deal more than single people.[20] Besides which, husbands and wives almost always leave their worldly goods— including pension benefits—to one another, creating the equivalent of an annuity for the surviving spouse. Given that wives tend to be younger than husbands, and women live an average of seven years longer than men, these annuities are most commonly enjoyed by women.[21]

Married people also tend to be healthier. According to a review article in the *Journal of Marriage and Family,* "The nonmarried have higher rates of mortality than the married, about 50 percent higher among women and 250 percent higher among men." Unmarried people (divorced, widowed, and never married) it turns out, are far more likely to die from a whole variety of causes—heart disease, pneumonia, cancer, car accidents, cirrhosis of the liver, and suicide. And this is true cross-culturally. In countries as different as Japan and the Netherlands, the unmarried die off much earlier than the married.

Single men tend to endanger their health by indulging in risky behavior—they drink and smoke too much, take drugs, drive dangerously, eat badly, and fail to get medical checkups. Single women are not nearly as careless or accident-prone, but they also are less healthy than their married peers because they miss out on the economic protection of marriage. Married women enjoy significantly higher household incomes than single women, and these higher incomes translate into better housing, safer neighborhoods, and improved access to private health insurance.

Finally we come to sex. Contrary to popular opinion—which tends to assume that swinging singles are the ones with the "hot" sex lives—married people have more and better sex than single people.[22] Over the last decade, several new studies, including The National Sex Survey—conducted at the University of Chicago and based on a sample of 3,500 adults—fill us in on what is happening. Fully 43 percent of married men report having sex at least twice a week, while only 26 percent of single men say they have sex this often. The picture is similar for women. Thirty-nine percent of married women have sex two or three times a week, compared to 20 percent of single women. In addition, both husbands and wives are more satisfied with sex than sexually active singles. The figures are particularly impressive for wives: 42 percent of married women say they find sex extremely emotionally and physically satisfying, compared to just 31 percent of single women.

The new research is quite startling in its clarity. Marriage can be an exceptionally good deal for both men and women. As might be expected, there are gender differences—men and women benefit in distinct and separate ways—but overall, married folks lead happier, healthier, and more prosperous lives than their single counterparts.

On the face of it this would seem like an extremely powerful set of findings, a treasure trove of important information for young people to sink their teeth into as they wrestle with challenging life decisions. The only problem is, very few people seem aware of this body of work on the benefits of marriage. None of the young women I interviewed knew anything about these studies. Even some of the "experts" I talked to—psychologists such as Bonnie Maslin—had barely heard of them.

Why hasn't this new research made more of a dent on our collective conscience? The answer to this question lies deep in our political culture.

There is enormous inertia around ideas, particularly ideas that help sustain a powerful ideology. Jessie Bernard's critique of marriage is a case in point. Once her analysis was accepted as "fact," it proved to be extremely useful in bolstering the feminist case against traditional marriage. And this, in turn, made her ideas exceedingly difficult to dislodge, even as times and circumstances have changed. So Bernard's analysis lives on, coloring if not distorting women's views on marriage. At least among the college-educated, it is the exceptional woman who does not have a lingering sense that marriage is bad for her, that it will pin her down and erode her potential.

Vivien Strong is such an exception. She stands out in my memory as one of the very few young women I interviewed who was thoroughly convinced that getting married would improve her life and was prepared to devote a great deal of time and energy to nurturing a relationship that might lead to marriage. Not that she had read the new research—along with most women I interviewed, she hadn't heard of it— but something in her background or makeup had insulated her from absorbing the skepticism around marriage which pervades our culture.

I met Vivien Strong, 29, in the spring of 2000 at a post-concert reception at Carnegie Hall. She was arm-in-arm with her brand-new, adoring husband, and when asked, talked almost apologetically about the next steps in her impressive career. It was quite clear from our brief initial conversation that if anyone was poised to "have it all," it might well be this young surgeon-in-training.

A few months later we got together for lunch, and after half an hour of pleasant conversation we edged into more personal territory. By dessert, Strong was ready to talk about herself:

"Getting married some time in my twenties was an enormously important goal for me, even stronger than my drive to succeed. I have always known that getting married reasonably young would make me happier and help me deal with life." She leaned forward in her chair, "but it was surprisingly hard to pull off."

There were times when finding a man seemed to be more difficult than becoming a surgeon. Looking back, it seems amazing to me, but I spent three years in medical school without dating at all. I was surrounded by all these guys, but none of them saw me as a potential date.

I've thought about this a lot. Doctors often have limited social skills and are under a lot of work-related stress, so they need a woman who has the time and patience to compensate and doesn't threaten them on other fronts. They therefore seek out less ambitious women: nurses, physical therapists, social workers. Women who are willing to put their work on a back burner, or even give it up entirely when they have kids. Obviously there are exceptions, but by and large, male doctors don't want the career challenge, the salary challenge, or the intellectual challenge that comes with dating a peer.

I'll never forget one man I dated just after I graduated from medical school. He wasn't a physician—I had given up on doctors by that time—but was an executive with one of the television networks. Well, despite the fact he was a successful, appealing person, he had a hard time with the fact that I had more degrees than he did—he was a college graduate but had no professional degrees. He kept on telling me that this career of mine was amazing, that I must be a genius. Over dinner one evening I remember him talking on and on about how I was dedicating my life to healing the sick—like a priest! It was so ridiculous it made me squirm. We only dated a couple of times because it was just too uncomfortable. I'm sure he didn't enjoy being overawed by me, and I didn't enjoy being put on a pedestal. At the time I thought it a great pity as we really liked one another. But I learned an important lesson: never date anyone who doesn't have a professional degree or a Ph.D. Men have a hard time with women who are more credentialed than they are.

Strong grew up in Wisconsin, a much beloved daughter in a traditional family. Her father was a successful surgeon and her mother was an enormously accomplished homemaker—she wallpapered, made curtains, landscaped, cooked, and sewed.

Strong attended Wellesley College and then Cornell Medical School. After earning her M.D., she was accepted into a surgical residency. When we met, she was three and a half years into a five-year residency and beginning to think through her career options. Given her stellar academic record, she was leaning toward combining a research job in a teaching hospital with private practice. She was well aware that surgical specialties are still heavily dominated by men—only 9 percent of assistant professors and 3 percent of full professors in this field are women—but was undaunted. Given her work ethic and track record, she felt she could bring it off.

By this point in our conversation I knew I was talking to an extremely determined young woman, but one who had had difficulties on the dating front. I was therefore immensely curious about her courtship and eventual marriage. Who was her husband? How had they met? And even more important, why had this relationship worked when others hadn't? According to Strong, it was pretty much love at first sight.

> Jim and I met through friends and right away I knew he might be the one for me. The attraction between us was amazing, and it didn't hurt that he had all the right characteristics. Jim is a lawyer-turned-businessman, highly credentialed, but not in the same field as I am. He is also a little older and therefore less likely to feel threatened. Not that I gave him much of a chance to feel intimidated by me. Given my experience with

that network executive, I leaned over backwards to be supportive and nonthreatening.

When we first started dating, this resolve of mine was really put to the test. Jim's dad had recently died and he was in the throes of taking over the family business. One of his initial challenges was getting to know the clients—to earn their confidence and make sure they understood he could handle their needs. What this seemed to boil down to was a never-ending series of business dinners—sometimes as many as four a week. Jim invited me to join him in hosting these dinners because many of his clients brought their wives and he thought my presence would make these evenings more successful.

I remember thinking: If I want this relationship to get off the ground I just have to figure out a way of standing by him and doing these dinners. The logistics were horrendous. I had just begun my surgical residency and was working about a hundred hours a week. The only way to pull off these dinners was to constantly juggle my schedule—trading hours with colleagues, doing additional back-to-back shifts—to free up evenings so I could rush off to a restaurant to act the gracious hostess. I have to say there were times when I would have preferred a long, hot bath. After a thirty-six-hour shift the last thing I needed was yet

another opportunity to spend two and a half hours
eating dinner with people I had never met before.

There was very little in these dinners for me.
Don't get me wrong, they weren't unpleasant. As
a doctor, I can always sustain a conversation
because people love talking about their aches and
pains—arthritic joints, weight-loss diets, prostate
cancer treatment, you name it. But looking back I
would say that none of these clients were people I
would have chosen to spend time with. The point
is, I was falling in love and I needed to go that
extra mile to show Jim that, despite my career, I
knew how to be a supportive and loyal partner.

Well, as you know, it all paid off.

Strong gave me a wide and glorious smile. "Jim was
incredibly grateful and I felt deeply appreciated. Those
dinners kind of turned us into a team. A year later we
were engaged and two years later we were married."[23]

Despite the obvious logic of her approach to life,
Vivien Strong is a long way from being typical of her
generation. She was able to make this marriage happen
because she planned for it. She planned for it in the
logistical sense of freeing up time and attention for
Jim. But she also planned for it in the deeper psychological sense of being willing to surrender part of her
own identity to enhance that of the man she wanted to
be with.

Most of the young women I interviewed for this book were simply not prepared to go that far in the name of marriage. They were worried about ending up divorced like their parents and preoccupied with the need to "figure themselves out" before committing to another person. But when push came to shove, they were also unprepared to make the sacrifices necessary to share a life with someone else. Strong was very clear about what she'd have to sacrifice in order to be married. By way of contrast, many of her peers seem to think that any relationship requiring sacrifice is, by definition, one that is flawed.

That is why the information contained in this chapter has the potential of being enormously helpful. It enables young women to cut through the anxiety and skepticism around marriage and figure out that giving priority to establishing a stable, loving relationship early on might well be worth the effort even if this involves surrendering part of one's own ego. The new research shows very clearly that when a woman gets and stays married (an extremely important proviso), many good things happen to her: she extends her life expectancy, increases her level of financial security, and enhances her sex life. But even more important from the vantage point of this book: she massively improves her chances of having a child. Despite the fact that women today can and do choose to raise children on their own, it is an uphill and difficult road. A

fact borne out in our survey. Only 3 percent of the
women in *High-Achieving Women, 2001* chose to bear
(or adopt) a child out of wedlock.

The day I interviewed Bonnie Maslin she had a
conceptual breakthrough:

> I'm so used to thirty-eight-year-old women
> behaving like twenty-eight-year-olds, and sixty-
> eight-year-old women behaving like fifty-eight-
> year-olds, that I had almost convinced myself that
> it didn't much matter. Women still spend the same
> thirty years in the prime of life.
>
> But delayed maturity matters a hell of a lot on
> the childbearing front. I know enough biology to
> understand that a woman is born with a finite
> number of eggs, and sometime in her late thirties
> or early forties she will begin to run out. No mat-
> ter how great she looks, no matter how much she
> spends on fertility treatments, she cannot change
> that biological reality. Delayed maturity means
> that a whole lot of women effectively "waste" their
> window of fertility.[24]

At that point an excited Bonnie Maslin began to draw
some lines on her living room couch. Using a fingernail,
she drew two crude graphs on the butter-colored velour
of a seat cushion, then sat back to admire her handiwork:

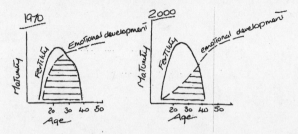

Methodogical elegance aside, Maslin had reason to be excited. Her crude graphs explain a great deal. As we see in chapter 5, the fact that a woman's physical and emotional development have gotten so out of sync spells disaster on the childbearing front. The struggle to develop an authentic identity—in work and in love—can be exceptionally protracted these days, and an accomplished woman who delays commitment and marriage can turn around and discover that she has inadvertently squandered her fertility.

5

INFERTILITY: THE EMPTY
PROMISE OF HIGH-TECH
REPRODUCTION

On a gray Sunday morning in Seattle, I am at a restaurant near the Pike Street market having brunch with Linda Davenport. Davenport was a student of mine in the late 1980s, and we have kept in touch ever since. Now 35, she is the marketing director of a fast-growing software company located on the edge of this trendy city. After the usual catch-up, she launches into the main event in her life. She has just broken up with Lance, her live-in boyfriend of four years. "He just couldn't take the fact that I work as hard as he does," she says. "His attitude was so unfair. I mean, if I got home and he was still at work, I was supposed to just deal with it. But if he got home and I was still at the office, he would get as resentful as hell. He just didn't want me to compete at the same level."

I make comforting and supportive noises, and, reacting to the sympathy, Davenport looks stricken. Carefully folding and refolding her table napkin, she struggles to keep back the tears. "Sundays are hard," she says softly.

A moment later she perks up and becomes animated again. "I always thought that if I got to be 35 and hadn't had a child, I would slit my wrists or something. But I really feel I can breathe easy on the kid front. With all these medical breakthroughs women can have children later and later. Did you read about this Italian woman who had one at 63? I think it's great, and it means I can put off having children until my forties. It's such a relief. I feel that I have been given an extra seven or eight years."[1]

If only it were that simple, if only a 35-year-old woman could wait, and in a leisurely fashion, launch a career and find the perfect mate before thinking about having children. The plain fact is, if Linda waits until she's 43 or 45 before attempting to have a child, she most probably will not have one.

In recent years, women have been sold a bill of goods on the fertility front. Misled by the media, which loves to hype miracle babies, and lulled into a false sense of security by an infertility industry eager to profit from late-in-life babies, too many young women now believe that assisted reproductive technology (ART) has let them off the hook. Like Davenport, they believe that the huge range of new options—IVF, GIFT, ZIFT, donor eggs, you name it—will allow them to push the difficult question of when and how to have a child into the distant future. They feel that they can quite literally "rewind the biological clock." Almost 90 percent of the 28–40-year-old women who participated in *High-Achieving Women, 2001* believed that ART would allow them to get pregnant into their forties.

Unfortunately, the optimism of Linda Davenport and the survey respondents is ill-founded. The average forty-something woman trying to get pregnant for the first time faces daunting odds no matter how hard she tries, no matter how much she spends. According to the research presented later on this chapter, a woman in her early 40s has, on average, a 3–5 percent shot at achieving a live birth through standard IVF procedures. Not only do women have an extremely hard time getting pregnant at these ages, but a 42- or 44-year-old woman who gets pregnant faces a 50–80 percent chance of losing her baby through miscarriage.

Donor eggs can significantly boost an older woman's chance at conception, but obtaining these precious eggs has its own set of challenges. Prices are high and rising rapidly (eggs start at $3,000 and can go all the way up to $50,000 for so-called designer eggs), and since the demand for eggs continues to exceed the supply, many clinics have long waiting lists and shut out older women.

These facts are hard to come by. Infertility in America has become a highly profitable multi-billion-dollar industry that likes to tout the good news. Fertility clinics have mushroomed in recent years (the number of clinics doubled between 1996 and 2000 and there are now more than 400 around the country). In the increasingly fierce competition for well-heeled patients some of the more discouraging facts are concealed or disguised. For example, clinics often inflate their success rates by suggesting that pregnancy rather than a live birth is the end goal. Since women in their forties face extremely high rates of miscarriage, this redefinition can more than double real success rates for older women.

Anne Newman, a writer at *Business Week*, now wishes that she and her husband had been better informed on the baby-making front:

> A few years ago, after more than three months
> of a healthy pregnancy, I had my fourth and final
> miscarriage. I was 45 years old. A lab report
> showed that the baby had been a boy with
> Down's syndrome. My husband, Paul, and I had

seen him on a sonogram just three weeks earlier.
He had the oversize head typical of a young fetus,
and his tiny hands were waving wildly. We fanta-
sized about bringing home a baby as robust as our
splendid three-year-old Elizabeth.

This was by far our hardest loss. We thought
we had gotten past the twelve-week mark and had
begun to believe in this baby. After the tissue came
back showing that the baby had Down's syndrome, I knew that we couldn't try again—that
this was the end of the line. I finally understood
the risks we were facing.

Paul and I believed technology was going to
help us conquer the odds. In a general sense, we
knew that a successful pregnancy became more
difficult with age, but when I got pregnant this
last time I had no idea that I had a 53 percent
chance of miscarriage and a 1 in 26 chance of having a child with chromosomal problems. I hadn't
done the research the way I should have.

Looking back on our experience, I am pretty
angry with my doctors. My obstetrician kept on
telling me that I was 'forty-five-years young' and
to keep on trying. There's such a gung ho attitude
out there. These infertility guys encourage women
to believe age is not a factor when, of course, it's
huge. They focus on their success stories and have
little interest in the heart-wrenching losses most of
us deal with. The pain wrapped up in those four

dead babies was—and is—almost unbearable.
After the first miscarriage we held a small,
private, memorial service and buried our child in
a Quaker cemetery. But we couldn't bear to bury
the other three. One day we must confront the
realities of those deaths.

I did not expect to fail on the baby-making
front. I fully intended to be a mother by age 30,
but my life did not turn out that way. I spent my
twenties and early thirties earning a living as a
freelance journalist specializing in Africa, which
made it difficult to settle down. Partly because of
this I went back to school to become a business
journalist. That's when I met my husband. But by
then I was thirty-seven years old.

Three years later I was a first-time bride with a
great job at *The Wall Street Journal*. Paul and I
planned to have children right away, and indeed I
got pregnant after just one month of trying—without fertility drugs. Pictures in our family album
show a grinning forty-year-old pointing to a positive pregnancy test. Two months later, a sonogram
showed I was carrying a dead fetus.

I will never forget the 1992 Democratic convention. Feet up, watching Clinton and company on
TV, I waited for my body to abort my first child,
and cried every time I saw a baby in a commercial
or on the convention floor. At 3:00 A.M. on the
morning of June 17, the fetus was expelled. As I

struggled to cope with my emotions, I dutifully collected the bloody tissue in a baggie for the hospital lab.

Like many other women, I tried to shrug off that first miscarriage. I quickly returned to my job and lost myself in work. Three months later I was pregnant again, after just one month on Clomid—a fertility drug to used to stimulate the release of eggs from the ovaries. This time my doctor prescribed progesterone to help fortify the lining of my uterus and support the growing fetus.

I ate like a horse and grew huge. After a text-book forty-two-week pregnancy, I delivered an eight-pound, thirteen-ounce Elizabeth just one month before my forty-second birthday. For a brief period in there, former classmates from the Columbia School of Journalism were calling me a role model for late-blooming, motherhood.

Inspired by Elizabeth, we planned to have another child. But other agendas intervened (my mother-in-law became terminally ill) and sixteen months rolled by before we attempted to conceive again. With a heavier dose of Clomid, it then took me five months to get pregnant. Two months later, a sonogram again delivered sad news: the fetus was lifeless.

After this loss, my doctor suggested that I seek treatment from a fertility specialist, so I began a more intensive fertility regime with Pergonal, a stronger drug than Clomid. Paul took on the chore of injecting the drug into my arm. Once again, I got pregnant. Once again I miscarried—this time after only six weeks.

Now I tell anyone who has a choice not to delay childbearing until their late thirties. I try to explain what happens to the odds—in terms of getting pregnant, staying pregnant, and bearing a healthy child. My advice to young women is: start thinking about kids in your early thirties, especially if you want to have more than one child. Do the research. Look at the statistics. You can avoid huge amounts of heartache if you start earlier than we did.

But as soon as I hand out that kind of advice I realize how hard it is to follow. Take my case. I was busy changing careers in my mid-thirties— I went back to get a graduate degree at Columbia when I was thirty-five. And I didn't meet the right man until I was thirty-seven—before then they were all turkeys.

So what can be done? At the very least, graduate schools should get involved. Neither Columbia nor any other school I know sponsors a course on how to combine career with family, and yet this has been the central challenge of my professional life. We need graduate schools to do this. It would encourage people—men and women—to plan better.[2]

Perhaps the most remarkable thing about reproductive technology and the supposed end of the biological clock is just how unrevolutionary the revolution has been.

The vast majority of women still have babies the old-fashioned way. In 1998, the most recent year for which statistics are available, 25,582 babies were born as a result of IVF (which accounts for most births through assisted reproductive technology). This figure accounts for only six-tenths of 1 percent of 3.9 million babies born that year. What is more, during that same year, a mere 3,624 babies were born to women over 45. Indeed, there were more babies born to women ages 45–49 thirty-five years ago than today.[3] This is because the profile of a woman who successfully carries a child to term in her mid- or late-forties is a married woman in good health who already has several children, not a single, childless woman like Wendy Wasserstein.

The media has made a meal out of the success stories. "Miracle Mom at 63! First Photos and Interview," screamed *The National Enquirer* on Mother's Day, 1997. The tabloid press told an eye-catching story.

Arceli Keh—who emigrated from the Philippines and now lives in Highland, a community 60 miles east of Los Angeles—got married in 1980 at the age of 47. She and her husband Isagani then tried to get pregnant but Keh soon plunged into menopause and began to realize that she had almost no chance of conceiving the child she longed for so much. Several years later she read about in vitro fertilization and lied about her age to get into the UCLA egg-donor program, where, in due course, she became pregnant and gave birth to an infant girl.

Baby Cynthia, born in December 1996, was a full-term baby and weighed six pounds at birth. The doctors described her as "healthy as a horse." Amazingly, this 63-year-old mom breast-fed her baby. Keh is impatient with those who voice anxiety about her age. She says she has many family members who have lived into their nineties so she's not concerned about the possibility of not seeing her daughter grow up. In fact, God willing, she'd love to give Cynthia a brother or sister, but has decided to wait until her daughter is in kindergarten (by which time Keh would be in her late sixties).

The Kehs are modest people. Isagani is a worker in a urethane foam factory and earns $24,000 a year, and yet the couple saved $32,000 to pay for the various in vitro fertilization treatments that eventually led to Cynthia's conception and birth. "I wasn't trying to make history," Arceli Keh told a British newspaper, "I just wanted a baby."

No wonder women like Linda Davenport latch on to this story—which was featured on the *Today Show* and splashed across every newspaper in America. The subliminal message is extraordinarily powerful: If cutting-edge reproductive technology allows an emigrant working-class woman to have a baby at age 63—and breast feed to boot—baby-making should be a cinch for affluent, well-educated white women in their forties. This seductive message is reinforced by airbrushed stories of middle-aged, celebrity moms favored by glossy magazines.

Hello magazine ran an admiring spread about Jane Seymour, star of the long-running television series *Dr. Quinn, Medicine Woman,* who became pregnant with twins at 44. Seymour and her husband, director James Keach, are pictured relaxing at their eighteenth-century manor house just outside of Bath. As they tell the story, they already had a house full of children by previous spouses, but when they got married they just had to have a child together. No problem. With the help of GIFT (gamete intra fallopian transfer, a variant of IVF) they managed to get pregnant. It wasn't all clear sailing: Seymour developed preeclampsia and as a result, the twins were born six weeks early. But the baby boys had very few problems. In fact they were so healthy—and so adorable—they became Gerber babies and appeared in print and television baby-food ads across the country.

People magazine featured Cheryl Tiegs on its cover. The 52-year-old former model was ecstatic because she and her husband, yoga master Rod Stryker, were expecting twins, courtesy of a surrogate mother. The couple started trying to get pregnant in 1998, but after several failed attempts at IVF, turned to a surrogate. "We found this angel who was willing to carry our baby," said Tiegs. Tiegs took fertility drugs to increase the number of eggs that could be harvested and fertilized. The resulting embryos were transferred to the surrogate's uterus and the procedure was successful on the very first try. "They're my eggs and my husband's sperm, so they're our babies," said Tiegs, who went on to say that she believed she would be an even better mother today than when she was younger.[4]

And *Talk* magazine published the story of Helen Morris, Martin Scorsese's fourth wife, who had her first child when she was 52—it turned out to be a breeze. According to this article, Morris—a Random House editor—just happened to be in the right place at the right time.

In 1995, just before she turned 50, she met Martin Scorsese in the course of editing a memoir by his friend, the late Michael Powell. Bingo. Two years later the happy couple were living together in Scorsese's sunny, book-lined town house, and a year after that they were the proud parents of baby Francesca.

As described in this magazine story, the baby-making part was amazingly straightforward. "I went to my gynecologist," Morris says, "and he thought I was a little old. A doctor in New York was recommended, someone who specialized in high-risk pregnancies, and I got pregnant immediately. I mean I was 51. I have Parkinson's. I was in bed for a few months, but it was easy. I watched a lot of television."[5]

Wait up. Don't we need a reality check here? Shouldn't the reader know how many 52-year-old women—let alone women with Parkinson's disease—can expect to coast through conception and pregnancy with such golden and glorious luck? At the very least this article might have come clean about some of the challenges even the lucky ones face. Take, for example, the price tag for IVF: over 90 percent of late-in-life pregnancies involve IVF, and prices range from $10,000 to $100,000, depending on how many attempts are required and whether or not you need donor eggs. And then there are those wretched Pergonal shots that accompany any IVF treatment. The ones that cause you to swell up like a blowfish and make your moods swing so wildly that you spend most afternoons in tears.

The Keh, Seymour, Tiegs, and Morris stories send a dangerous message: that women can wait to have children because technology will be there to save them when they are ready. But for every 52-year-old woman who succeeds, thousands more waste an inordinate amount of energy, time, and money. The sobering reality is that over a ten-year period (1989–1999) fewer than 200 American women over 50 succeeded in having a baby.

So what is the real deal?

If you take away the hype and the hard sell, what are the chances that an older woman can get pregnant in this age of Assisted Reproductive Technology (ART)? And what risks does she face, both in terms of her own health and the health of her prospective baby?

First of all, 63-year-old, first-time moms notwith-standing, age continues to be a huge problem for women who want children. It's true that women today are healthier and live much longer than women in pre-vious generations, but overall they are somewhat less fertile than their mothers were, even factoring in the impact of new technologies. Contemporary women are likely to have had several sexual partners and therefore experience a much higher incidence of pelvic inflam-matory disease, which creates scar tissue that can block the fallopian tubes. They also routinely miss out on the prime childbearing years—ages 20–30. The net result: higher rates of infertility.

Fertility rates begin to drop after age 30, then plunge after age 35. According to figures put out by the Mayo Clinic, peak fertility occurs between ages 20 and 30. Fertility drops 20 percent after age 30, 50 percent after age 35, and 95 percent after age 40. While 72 percent of

28-year-old women get pregnant after trying for a year, only 24 percent of 38-year-olds do.

This drastic fall-off in fertility can come as a devastating shock. "I can't tell you how many people we've had on our help line, crying and saying they had no idea how much fertility drops as you age," says Diane Aronson, a former executive director of RESOLVE, a support network for women and men coping with infertility and loss. "The message needs to get out that reproduction is much more difficult with age."

The basic problem is that women run out of eggs. A baby girl is born with all the eggs she will ever have— several hundred thousand, stored in her ovaries. Each month the ovaries release eggs and the supply is gradually depleted until menopause, when no eggs are left. In the words of Dr. Cristina Matera, assistant professor of clinical obstetrics and gynecology at New York Presbyterian Medical Center, "What women don't understand is that although they look great feel great and live energetic lives, their ovaries are still aging."[6]

Advancing age is not the only cause of infertility. Approximately six million American women and their partners are infertile, and only a minority of these couples are dealing with age-related infertility. Common medical problems are a blocked fallopian tube or a low sperm count, and for these situations the new techniques of assisted reproductive technology are enormously effective. ART is much less helpful with age-related problems. Dr. Zev Rosenwaks, director of the Center for Reproductive Medicine and Infertility at New York Hospital–Cornell Medical Center, is very clear on the subject: "If you are over forty, ART is unlikely to solve your infertility problem."[7]

But let's back up for a moment. What precisely is ART?

The first thing to know is that there are different types of assisted reproductive technology. Many couples start with one of the simpler technologies and, if that fails, they "graduate" to a more expensive and invasive technology. The progression usually goes like this: If a couple fails to conceive after a year of trying, a doctor first recommends a course of hormone therapy to see if merely stimulating the ovaries to produce more eggs might solve the problem. If this doesn't work, the couple may then elect to try in vitro fertilization (IVF)—the treatment of choice for age-related infertility.

IVF, which costs approximately $12,000 per cycle, entails a series of complicated steps. First, a woman takes a combination of the drugs Lupron and Pergonal to stimulate egg production, which puts her in a state of hyperovulation or superovulation. Her ovaries are closely monitored by ultrasound and blood hormone tests to make sure the eggs are maturing. Then, before natural ovulation occurs, a needle-tipped probe guided by ultrasound is inserted through the vaginal wall into the ovary, and the mature eggs are removed and placed in an incubator with prepared sperm. Fertilization can then occur. After two to eight cell divisions, which take about two days, several of these "pre-embryos" are inserted into the woman's uterus using a catheter. Two weeks later she takes a blood test to see if she is pregnant.

How successful is IVF for women in older age brackets? The figures are extremely discouraging.

Since 1992 the American Society for Reproductive Medicine (ASRM) has tracked success rates in infertility clinics around the nation. The ASRM data for 1999—the most recent year available—show that women 35 years old or younger have a 28 percent chance of getting pregnant and achieving a live birth as a result of a single IVF cycle. By age 39 the success rate drops to 8 percent per cycle, and by age 44 it falls to 3 percent. The ASRM data are confirmed by a more recent study (September 2000) which analyzes success rates among 431 women who attempted ART in their forties. A mere 4.5 percent of these women succeeded in having a child (a more pertinent outcome than getting pregnant), and all of the success stories occurred in the 41–43 age group. The authors of this study recommend that doctors not treat patients older than 44.[8]

Even if a woman in her forties is able to conceive through ART, she then runs a daunting set of risks. The most well known is an increased likelihood that the child will suffer from Down's syndrome—a combination of mental retardation and physical abnormality. At age 25 a woman has a 1 in 1,250 chance of having a baby with Down's syndrome; at age 45 she has a 1 in 26 chance. In recent years this chromosomal disorder has become much less problematic for women over 35 because a common prenatal test now diagnoses or rules out Down's syndrome.

Much more serious is the risk of miscarriage. It has long been known that older women have miscarriage rates that are higher than average because they are more likely to have genetically flawed eggs that fail to implant properly. A new study determines just how high these rates are. A Danish study which appeared in the June 2000 issue of the *British Medical Journal* found that in older age groups, over half the pregnancies ended in fetal loss.[9] The study, based on a sample of 600,000 women, clearly linked miscarriage to the age of the mother. At age 22 a pregnant woman faces an 8 percent chance of losing her baby through miscarriage, but at age 48 that possibility increases to 84 percent.

The study also found that older women are much more at risk for multiple births.

The incidence of "supertwins" (triplets and more) has quadrupled since the mid-1980s, primarily as an unintended side-effect of infertility treatment. Either too many embryos are transferred during an IVF cycle, or the ovaries are supercharged by a strong fertility drug such as Pergonal and release eight or ten eggs all at once, and these eggs have the potential of becoming eight or ten babies. Older women are disproportionately at risk for a multifetal pregnancy because they are more aggressively treated by infertility specialists.

When we read about cute, cuddly supertwins who survive and thrive—the 1999 McCaughey septuplets are a case in point—it's easy to forget that quints and septuplets usually turn into a medical tragedy. Louis Keith, director of the Chicago-based Center for the Study of Multiple Births becomes agitated when talking about the media image of multiple births. The babies are "buffed, toned, airbrushed, and made to look wonderful. What distorts the issue is that the press is very eager to do a story on a mother of quints, all of whom are four pounds or more, but they don't find it very newsworthy to describe cases where the babies are born very prematurely and die one by one."[10]

In a 1991 statement, the Ethics Committee of the American College of Obstetricians and Gynecologists urged doctors to warn infertility patients prior to treatment about the "dire consequences" of multifetal pregnancies. "These situations get sensationalized in the media as this great thing when, in fact, it's a medical disaster," said Dr James Grifo, the head of New York University Medical Center's division of reproductive endocrinology.[11]

In 1998, Pam Belluck wrote a story for *The New York Times* about parents who've had multiple births:

> Like so many other parents, they sent out a birth notice, Mario and Jane Simmone proudly announce the birth of their new arrivals. It listed the names of their triplets, the birth weights, lengths and birth date: June 21, 1997.
>
> Color photographs depicted what words could not: Amber Raquel in the yellow light of a neonatal incubator; Cheyenne Barbara with tubes sprouting from chest, legs, arms, and hands; Mario Victor with a ventilator tube taped to his mouth.
>
> Next to Amber's photograph was another vital statistic: "deceased, June 24, 1997." Next to Cheyenne's the caption read "deceased July 6, 1997." By the time the announcements were mailed only Mario Jr. was still alive.[12]

The reality of high-order multiples (three or more infants) can be brutal. The children are often dangerously premature; many weigh less than three pounds, four ounces—the official definition of a very low birth weight baby (VLBW). A significant proportion of VLBW babies—perhaps 10–20 percent—die during the first year of life. For the tiny survivors the long term can be darkened by cerebral palsy, and a host of less obvious disabilities. There is now a weight of evidence showing that VLBW infants experience significant health problems. They suffer from recurrent infections, frequent hospitalizations, and lag behind their peers in most areas of physical, cognitive, and behavioral development.

A study published in *Pediatrics* in February 2000 followed 150 babies who were born weighing two pounds or less and showed that the fallout from very low birth weight can be lifelong, for the parents as well as the babies.[13] By their early teens, many of these children had significant physical disorders including cerebral palsy, blindness, and deafness. A high proportion also experienced difficulties in school. Nearly half were receiving special-education assistance compared with 10 percent in a control group of children who were born full term. In May 2000, Sheryl Gay Stolberg wrote about one low birth weight child in the *The New York Times:*

It has been 11 years since Alex Martin was born, a 1-pound 2-ounce bundle of miniature bones and bright red skin, with fingers no bigger than matchsticks and legs so thin they might have fit inside his father's wedding band.

Today, Alex is a blond-haired, fair-skinned fifth grader with . . . a collection of what his mother calls labels: mild cerebral palsy, asthma, hyperactivity, and Asperger's Syndrome, a form of autism. At an age when most children have conquered fractions, Alex wrestles with addition . . . Alex cannot ride a bike. He still wears sneakers that fasten with Velcro, because his fingers cannot master the intricacies of laces. "Life," Mrs. Martin says, "is overwhelming for him."

It is also overwhelming, at times, for his parents . . . Long after their worries about simply keeping Alex alive have faded, the Martins are faced with new and no less daunting concerns, from whether their son will ever be able to make change at the grocery store, or drive a car or maintain a job, to who will care for him after they die.[14]

Perhaps the most ominous threat posed by infertility treatment is an increased risk of cancer for the woman. Scientists have long been aware that many cancers— particularly those affecting the reproductive organs (breast, ovary, uterus, prostate) are exacerbated by exposure to hormones. As early as 1989, Dr. Florence Haseltine, then director of the Center for Population Research at the National Institutes of Health, sounded a warning at a convention of fertility specialists. "Everyone looks at risks of cancer from oral contraceptives, but what about these fertility drugs?" she asked the group.[15]

In 1993, these risks received greater attention with the publication of a study by Dr. Alice Whittemore of Stanford University that found that women who had been treated for infertility were three times more likely to develop ovarian cancer than women who had not been.[16]

Whittemore's study was greeted by an uproar. Women being treated with infertility drugs panicked, and the specialists treating them were seriously alarmed. Some experts in the field tried to discredit Whittemore, accusing her, among other things, of being a third-rate scientist. The president of ASRM sent a memo to member doctors describing her study as "seriously flawed," while one leading British fertility expert said, "The [Whittemore] paper is widely recognized as an extremely poor study. There is very little reason to suppose there is a link between infertility treatment and cancer."

After the uproar died down, even Whittemore herself saw her investigation as inconclusive. She speculated that the infertile women in her study may have had an underlying defect in their ovaries that both prevented them from getting pregnant and brought about malignancies. And she was the first to admit that the study did not distinguish between different types of infertility—for example, women with blocked fallopian tubes were clumped together with women whose husbands had low sperm counts.

The Whittemore study clearly had methodological problems but it was followed by several more rigorous studies that showed at least an association between infertility treatment and cancer. In 1994, Dr. Mary Anne Rossing looked at 4,000 women who were treated for infertility in the '70s and '80s and found that those who had taken Clomid for 12 or more cycles increased their risk of developing ovarian cancer eleven-fold.[17]

Two more recent studies failed to establish a strong link between infertility treatment and cancer. A 1999 study published by *The Lancet,* which looked at 29,000 Australian women who had taken infertility drugs in the '80s and '90s, demonstrated only a "transient" initial increase in the risk of developing breast or uterine cancer—detectable in the first year after treatment.[18] And a 1999 study published in *Fertility and Sterility* that looked at 1,197 Israeli women failed "to confirm an association between use of fertility drugs and an increased risk of breast or ovarian cancer."[19] However, as various experts have pointed out, this Israeli study dealt with an extremely small sample of women and therefore is limited in its usefulness.

Thankfully, more comprehensive studies are in the works. The National Cancer Institute, for example, is sponsoring a study involving some 100,000 women treated in infertility clinics over a thirty-year period, but its results are at least three years away.

Meanwhile, experts in the field warn women and their doctors to be more cautious. In the words of a recent editorial in *Fertility and Sterility*, "Biological theory and epidemiologic evidence support the possible association between infertility treatment and ovarian cancer . . . therapeutic protocols should therefore be shortened and women who have been treated with these drugs should be monitored more rigorously."[20]

This low-key, careful language is cold comfort to women dealing with the brutal reality of ovarian cancer. Many are bitter and angry, firm in their conviction that their cancers were caused by infertility treatments and that they had been used as "lab rats" by doctors seeking a quick route to fame and fortune. In her recent autobiography, Liz Tilberis, former editor of *Harper's Bazaar,* describes her battle with ovarian cancer. Zapped with megadoses of chemotherapy, reduced to an almost animal level of survival by a bone-marrow transplant, she writes: "Every day brought some new horrifying change to my body. My mouth became ulcerated and I couldn't swallow my own saliva. So I was given a small device to vacuum out my mouth. I knew I was dribbling, but I didn't care. The worst of it was the shaking chills—uncontrollable shivers, which got bigger and bigger, like an epileptic seizure."[21]

Over her five-year struggle with cancer Tilberis had plenty of time to reflect on its origins. She identified two sources: the sexual revolution and ART. Ironically, both revolutions were meant to create new freedom and new choices for women, not pain and terminal illness.

> My generation ushered in the sexual revolution, but it wasn't so revolutionary for me. I had exactly two sexual partners before Andrew and I met and mated for life, like swans. But somehow during my extremely nonswinging single days, I got PID—pelvic inflammatory disease. I didn't know it at the time. I only knew I had a yeast infection, called thrush in England. I went to a clinic where I was given yellow pessaries to deal with the itch. Yeast can mask other, more ominous kinds of sexually transmitted infections, and you don't have to be promiscuous to get one—just unlucky. Without knowing, I had developed a vaginal infection that spread to my fallopian tubes

and became salpingitis, a PID that ultimately
made me infertile.

Ten years later when Tilberis tried to get pregnant, she
discovered that both of her fallopian tubes were completely blocked from the salpingitis. Each tube is only
a few millimeters in diameter, so bacteria from an
infection can make the inner walls literally glue
together. Desperate to have a child, Tilberis under-
went major surgery in which one ovary and one of her
tubes were removed and the other tube cleared. To
her intense disappointment, she still failed to get pregnant and at this point decided to try IVF. She and her
husband went through a total of nine IVF cycles, each
cycle accompanied by megadoses of Pergonal. Eighteen
months later, numb, weary, broke, and still not pregnant, they called a halt to the debilitating process.
When Tilberis was diagnosed with ovarian cancer
many years later, she was certain her disease resulted
from "blasting" her ovaries with fertility drugs. After a
valiant five-year battle, Tilberis died in the spring of
1999, leaving behind a husband and two young,
adopted sons.

Which brings us to a critical question.

Why aren't these terrible risks—of miscarriage, of
multifetal pregnancy, of cancer—better known? And if
there's a cover-up, who are the bad guys?

Well, doctors are probably not the villains. At least not directly. The ones I've interacted with—as a patient and a researcher—are impressively credentialed, dedicated guys (most are men) with an infectious enthusiasm for their high-tech tools. None of these men seem irresponsible or grasping. But the fact is, you need to be a saint not to be affected by the market-driven pressures of ART in America. If there is a bad guy, it's the U.S. government, which has been conspicuous in its failure to regulate or oversee the infertility industry. Unlike governments in other countries, the U.S. government has failed to prohibit some of the riskier procedures, failed to either rein in or underwrite treatment costs, and failed to publicize the dangers attached to infertility treatment.

Take the problem of multiple births, about which there is an impressive measure of agreement among the experts. To use the words of Professor George Annas, chairman of the health law department at Boston University, "High-order multiples ought to be avoided . . . it's a preventable catastrophe."[22] But all too often, money gets in the way.

This is how it happens. The pregnancy rate achieved by an infertility clinic has an enormous impact on its ability to attract patients and thus on its bottom line. Doctors therefore are under intense pressure to bump up the number of embryos transferred in any IVF cycle to increase the likelihood that some of them will implant successfully. The ASRM recommends that the number of embryos transferred in any one cycle be limited to three or four (depending on the age of the woman), but doctors are not obligated by law to stick to this guideline, and many do not.

The problem is exacerbated by the fact that individual parents-to-be are under enormous financial pressure to get pregnant quickly.[23] As Anne Adams Lang wrote in *The New York Times,* "after four frustrating years not getting pregnant, Marianne Jornlin and her husband, Kris, embarked on high-tech reproduction. The couple, both software engineers, borrowed half of the $12,000 it costs for a single IVF cycle from Kris's parents and came home with quadruplets, now 19 months old." As Mrs. Jornlin told Lang, "Everything depended on that one cycle. The doctors gave me a 30 percent chance of a live birth. Where are you going to get the money for another cycle?"

In Lang's words, "Without insurance to defray costs, the Jornlins maximized the odds of succeeding in one try. Four of five healthy embryos were transferred into Mrs. Jornlin's womb. 'We were gung ho to do all five,' Jornlin said. 'The doctor had to restrain us.'

"Like virtually all parents who longed for, and, at last, have children, Mrs. Jornlin considers herself and her husband 'incredibly blessed.' Still, she admitted, 'I think now, going through all of this, if insurance had covered it, it would have been better to transfer two.'"[24]

Because they are dealing with intense emotional as well as financial pressure, infertility patients tend to push their doctors who, because of their own market-driven pressures, find it hard to push back. Which is where government needs to come in. The only way to ensure that doctors "push back" against market forces is to create an effective set of government regulations. Already, there are proposals for how this might be done. Arthur Caplan of the Center for Bioethics at the University of Pennsylvania suggests that the number of embryos planted in a woman's uterus be legally restricted so as to make "supertwins" much less likely. This restriction is already in place in many European countries.[25] He also proposes establishing a licensing body to accredit ART specialists. Currently, any doctor, no matter what his or her training, can set up shop as an infertility specialist. In Caplan's eyes, "The field needs oversight from top to bottom . . . reproductive technology is the closest thing we have right now to the Wild West."[26]

The reason the U.S. government has not acted to regulate this multibillion dollar industry is tied into the highly charged political battles around abortion. Back in the 1980s, the Reagan and Bush administrations,

prodded by the religious right, "instituted and main-
tained a de facto moratorium on government-sponsored IVF research because embryos might be
destroyed in the process" and thus got out of the business of both research and regulation.[27] As pointed out
by Dr. Benjamin Younger, executive director of
ASRM, "If we'd been doing the research, we might
have looked to develop some protocols on how to best
use these drugs, protocols that would have reduced the
risks . . . the dearth of research has left a great void in
this country."[28]

It's ironic that a conservative move to deny federal
funding for research on human embryos—due to "a
respect for life"—has succeeded in creating new forms
of risk for both women and their unborn children. By
demanding government inaction, conservatives have
ensured that American women who seek infertility
treatments are left to the tender mercies of the mar-
ketplace—with predictable consequences.

Desperate men and women—at least some of them
with deep pockets—and an unregulated market. This
is a combustible mix. And nowhere is this more evident
than in the burgeoning egg-donor business.

For more than a decade women who cannot produce
eggs themselves (primarily because they are too old,
but sometimes for other reasons) have sought to
become pregnant with donor eggs. The medical proce-

dure is the same as IVF, only the eggs are retrieved from another woman—called an egg donor—who is often paid handsomely for her eggs.

Becoming an egg donor is onerous. It typically takes six weeks to prepare a woman to donate her eggs. First, she undergoes a battery of medical tests to make sure she is healthy. Then she is injected with fertility drugs to stimulate her ovaries to produce many eggs. The growth of the eggs is monitored by a daily sonogram, which requires a trip to a doctor or clinic. When the eggs are ready for transplantation, the donor is partially anesthetized and a needle is inserted through the vagina into the ovaries to extract the eggs.

When egg-donor programs first got off the ground in the late 1980s, fertility clinics selected donors extremely carefully.[29] They screened candidates rigorously using a battery of physical and psychological tests, paid modest fees so as not to distort decision making, and limited the pool of potential donors to married women who had already completed their families. With such restrictions in place, however, supply did not keep pace with demand, and soon there were long waiting lists for donors. In response to the needs of affluent, older couples who chafed at losing precious time, at least some clinics became more aggressive and began raising the fees they paid egg donors and relaxing screening standards.

The surging demand for eggs also stimulated new developments in the market. A new breed of middleman, called an egg broker, emerged. Some merely charge a high fee for finding a prescreened, ready-to-go egg donor, thus enabling an infertile couple to jump the line. Others, like Ron Harris, offer designer eggs.

In October 1999, fashion photographer and Playboy channel film director Ron Harris started a website (Ronsangels.com) that features beautiful fashion models willing to auction their eggs—for the right price. Each webpage displays a sultry photograph of the potential donor along with her vital statistics. Infertile couples interested in the eggs of a particular woman can click on a link and make a bid online.

They might choose model number 462, who is a stunning 22-year-old blond with green eyes. A former child model for the Wilhelmina model agency, she is small and delicately built (height 5'3", weight 100 pounds) with perfect proportions (34B, 24, 32). The opening bid on her eggs is $90,000. Or they might choose model number 55, an extremely pretty 32-year-old brunette. Taller than number 462 (height 5'8", weight 130 pounds) this former model again has perfect proportions (36B, 26, 32).[30] Number 55 is a little heavier and a little older than the ideal, and her eggs are, relatively speaking, a bargain— opening bid a mere $20,000.

In an interview, Harris described how his new business feeds off the allure of beauty. "Just watch television and you will see we are only interested in looking at beautiful people. From network anchors to supermodels, our society is obsessed with looks. So if you can't have your own genetic child, then, of course you want to be in the market for the most beautiful eggs. But beauty will cost you."[31]

As we have seen, Harris's designer eggs carry hefty price tags, with opening bids ranging from $20,000 to $150,000. The models receive the full amount of the final bid. Ron then adds on a 20 percent commission. In addition, the infertile couple is responsible for all medical bills. Ron merely sells the eggs; he provides no medical services. Retrieving the eggs from the model donor plus the IVF procedure can run an additional $15,000. So if an infertile couple goes the route of designer eggs the complete package can easily cost $100,000. What do they get for this? A 40 percent shot at a clinical pregnancy (one detectable by a blood test in the very early stages), a 20 percent shot at a live birth, and a much smaller shot at a "model" baby. Gene pools are large and these babies are unlikely to look a whole lot like their beautiful mothers.

When word of Harris's website surfaced, it was met with a firestorm of criticism. People were outraged that someone with no medical training could set up shop on the Internet as a high-priced egg broker. "You can't run a blood donation center without a license, but you can set up your own egg brokerage service!" fumed Annette Lee, a reproductive endocrinologist at IVF New Jersey.

But Harris has his defenders, foremost among them other egg brokers. "People come to our service because they're frustrated—they're having trouble finding the right eggs," says Darlene Pinkerton, 47, whose high-end, egg-brokerage business at the San Diego law firm, Hill & Pinkerton, specializes in brains, not beauty. Pinkerton upped the ante on egg donor prices when she ran an ad in Ivy League college newspapers offering $50,000 for the right eggs.

"Egg-Seeking Ad Attracts Nearly 30 Harvard Applicants" blared the *Harvard Crimson* in July 1999. The article reported that the $50,000 offer convinced 28 Harvard students to answer a splashy ad seeking an egg donor for an infertile couple.

The solicitation, which ran in the *Harvard Crimson,* the *Stanford Daily,* and five other college newspapers, raised eyebrows and ethical concerns due to the huge sum of money involved and the specificity of the couple's requirements. They sought an "intelligent, athletic woman, 5'10" or over, with SAT scores of at least 1400.

All told, about 90 qualified candidates completed applications. Darlene Pinkerton, the couple's lawyer, said she received over 300 initial inquiries about the ad, but that the field got smaller after candidates received information describing the complicated medical procedure required.

"It explains what the retrieval process is," Pinkerton told the *Crimson* in the summer of 1999. "That's the point when we get a lot of attrition. Egg donors take hormones to boost their egg production before undergoing minor surgery to have the eggs removed." Pinkerton went on to say that she was surprised at the number of respondents. An earlier ad for the same couple, promising a "large financial incentive," but without a dollar figure, did not attract much interest.

Dr. Barry Behr, director of the IVF laboratory at Stanford Hospital, cautions couples who think that premium eggs donated by an Ivy League student will produce a whiz kid. "It's naive and ignorant to think you can buy intelligence," he says. "That just reflects a desperate desire to get a child of your dreams. How many professors have kids who don't become professors? How many kids don't follow in their parents' footsteps?"[32]

In this strange new world of egg brokers and big money, one thing seems clear: all kinds of inappropriate donors are being pulled into the net. Dr. Mark Sauer, director of the Center for Women's Reproductive Care at Columbia University, recalls how "ten years ago the idea that a young, unmarried women who had never been pregnant would undergo ovarian hyperstimulation and egg retrieval was unthinkable. With the risks of these invasive procedures far outweighing any benefit to donors, no ethics committee would have approved such a proposal." Sauer goes so far as to accuse his colleagues of "pimping for patients in need of eggs."[33]

The most serious risk faced by an egg donor is ovarian hyperstimulation syndrome—a complication of superovulation that leads to fluid buildup in the chest and abdomen and can result in kidney failure and even death. Donors also face other less serious risks that include ovarian infection, vaginal laceration, and a possible increase in the risk of ovarian cancer. Dr. Florence Haseltine of the National Institutes of Health has been a vocal critic. "There's no excuse for young girls to be getting drugs to donate eggs. How do we know their fertility won't be impaired? How do we know they won't go into early menopause? We are, after all, sticking their ovaries with needles."[34]

Emily, a graduate student who donated eggs in 1998, is now pondering these questions. "I was sort of led to believe that this is an incredibly low-risk procedure, that something mildly bad happens to one in 10,000 women," she said.[35] But the hormones pushed Emily's ovaries too far. She produced over 50 eggs and ended up hospitalized with ovarian hyperstimulation syndrome. When she got home, she was unable to walk up the stairs for weeks.

It turned out that Emily's doctors had an incentive to push her. The clinic they work for offers a shared-risk plan, meaning that patients pay a one-time fee for multiple IVF attempts—as many as it takes to get pregnant. What this means for the doctors is that they are paid only if the IVF attempt succeeds. They therefore have a huge incentive to bump up the number of eggs retrieved and transferred.

Despite this troubling story, the debate over egg donorship is not entirely black and white. In the United States an unregulated market is increasingly able to come up with eggs—even "beautiful," "smart" eggs!—for couples willing to pay for them. The downside is that at least some donors are placed at risk. In Europe, where markets are regulated, donors are not allowed to charge a fee, and, as a result, donors are nearly impossible to find.[36] Donors don't get seduced by large sums of money, but an infertile couple can expect to wait three to five years for an egg donor and many can't even get on the waiting lists because strict guidelines govern who is eligible for these scarce eggs. Some countries, most notably Canada and Israel, go so far as to outlaw the use of even volunteer egg donors.

Dr. Kamal Ahudja, head of the IVF Fertility Centre at the Cromwell Hospital in London, supports regulation of the donor market. "The safety of egg donors must assume priority over all other considerations,

including lack of donors," he says.[37] But it is a complicated ethical terrain. Whose interests are more important? Older women desperate for a child, or younger
women who could endanger their health by donating
eggs? Further muddying the waters is the fact that
many young women are eager to step into the breach
because they need the money—often to pay college
debts.

Putting these ethical issues aside for a moment, what
does this new egg market do to age-related infertility?
Can egg donation solve the fertility problems of older
women—or at least affluent older women? The answer
is a qualified no.

First the good news: donor eggs work. For women
over 40, the odds of getting pregnant and having a
child are much higher with donor eggs than with standard IVF procedures. Success rates—measured in
terms of live births—hover around the 20–25 percent
mark, which is five times the success rate achieved by
standard IVF for this age group. The problem is that
donor eggs come loaded with difficulties that run the
gamut from money to religion.

First, there is the daunting price tag. Even if a couple avoids egg brokers and waits patiently in line at an
infertility clinic, the cost of donor eggs plus one IVF
cycle is likely to be in the $15,000–$20,000 range.

Second, there are the emotional challenges. Many

women yearn for their own genetic child, and for them the decision to become pregnant with another woman's egg is often a last resort—the end of the line. In the words of one medical practitioner, "Many couples agree to try a donated egg only after great anguish, hacking their way through a thicket of difficult questions: How will the mother's relationship with the child be affected by the fact that she has no genetic tie? Should the parents reveal the child's unusual heritage to grandparents? Friends? The child? And when?"

Third, there continue to be real problems of access. Many older women find themselves shut out because of their age. Most clinics have an age ceiling in their egg-donor program that is only slightly higher than in their regular IVF program. For example, at Cornell the age ceiling is 44 in the regular IVF program and 46 in the egg-donor program. If a woman comes to egg donation as a last resort, having already exhausted all the other options, this two-year window gives her very little time. This is especially true if she cannot afford to use an egg broker and has to wait in line. At Cornell, for example, couples face a 12-month wait for an egg donor.

The age ceilings established at Cornell seem fairly typical of the industry. New York University Medical Center has exactly the same age cutoffs, while the St. Barnabas Medical Center in Livingston, N.J., and the

USC Fertility Group in Los Angeles give women one more year. In the New York City area, only Columbia-Presbyterian allows women over 50 to enroll in its egg-donation program.

Lurking behind these strict age limits are a set of disturbing medical realities. The USC group that pioneered postmenopausal pregnancy (63-year-old Arceli Keh was a patient in this program) has reported surprisingly high rates of obstetric complications in pregnant women aged 50 to 59. A USC study that followed 52 women—36 of whom got pregnant and 17 of whom delivered babies—found high rates of hypertension, preeclampsia, gestational diabetes, miscarriage, and multiple births.[38]

This is a fast-moving field and any number of medical breakthroughs are on the horizon. However, none of the new technologies are likely to radically change the odds facing women in their forties. For the foreseeable future this will remain a field where, to use the words of Dr. Mark Sauer, "failure is more commonly the norm."[39] Increasingly, experts in the field are advising women who want children not to wait too long. In September 2001 the American Society for Reproductive Medicine (ASRM) launched a bold new advertising campaign on city buses across the nation. The headline: "Advancing Age Decreases Your Ability to Have Children." The image: an upside-down baby bottle in the shape of an hourglass. "It's kind of like issuing a warning," says ASRM president Dr. Michael Soules. "It's our duty to let people know."[40]

Not everyone is happy with these ads, including Kim Gandy, president of the National Organization for Women, who sees them as creating unnecessary pressure on women. But what Gandy sees as unwelcome pressure, others see as essential knowledge that helps women get what they want in life. No one is clearer on this point than Dr. Zev Rosenwaks. In his words: "If you can try to become pregnant at a younger age you should. You're likely to get pregnant more often and earlier. You're likely to have a healthier pregnancy because you're less likely to have a miscarriage and less likely to have chromosomal abnormality. You're likely to have as many children as you want."[41]

Before leaving this chapter I want to put the peculiarly modern problem of delayed childbearing in proper perspective. Children—having them, not having them—have always been a huge deal in the lives of women. The fact is that throughout history, infertility has been a curse, and fertility has often been an even bigger curse.

The Bible is replete with older, childless women imploring God to give them a child. Sarah, Rebekah, Rachel, Elizabeth, and Hannah were all barren and deeply pained by their inability to have children. "Hannah was deeply distressed and prayed to the Lord, and wept bitterly. She made a vow, 'O Lord of hosts, if only you will look on the misery of your servant, and remember me, and not forget your servant, but will give to your servant a male child, then I will set him before you as a Nazarite until the day of his death.'"

Women in the Bible were prepared to go to enormous lengths to obtain a child; some even encouraged their husbands to impregnate slave girls or maids.

> When Rachel saw that she bore Jacob no children, she envied her sister; and she said to Jacob "Give me children, or I shall die!" Jacob became very angry with Rachel and said, "Am I in the place of God, who has withheld from you the fruit of the womb?" Then she said, "Here is my maid Bilhah; go in to her, that she may bear upon my knees and that I too may have children through her."[42]

But if infertility was a scourge, fertility was an even bigger burden. However much a woman might yearn for a child, bearing one might literally maim or kill her. Until the medical advances of the nineteenth century— Edward Lister's discovery of antisepsis in 1867 was particularly significant—baby-making for women was "a litany of torn bodies, blood and pain."[43]

In premodern times the average woman endured

eight pregnancies, six live births, and faced a 10 percent chance of dying in childbirth (fully a quarter of female deaths in women aged 15–50 were due to obstetrical causes). Among those who survived childbirth, many were so ripped apart during labor and delivery that they were crippled for the rest of their lives. The final coup de grace: A large proportion of these hard-won babies died. Up until the beginning of the nineteenth century, a woman could expect that at least two of her children would die before the age of five.

In his remarkable book, *Women's Bodies,* Canadian historian Edward Shorter pieces together what child-birth did to women in premodern Europe and North America based on letters, diaries, and other historical documents of the period.[44]

Long, drawn-out, difficult labors—up to 50 hours— were common. The underlying reason was often an overly small maternal pelvis (due to rickets or malnu-trition), which made it necessary for the child's head to force its way through an impossibly narrow birth canal. These protracted labors often became public events as the village community pitched in. Friends and neighbors would try and force the fetus out by shaking the mother or turning her upside down. Different cultures dealt with the problem in different ways. In France, mothers were tied upside down on a ladder. In Ireland, when labor seemed to be taking too long, two or three large men would shake the unhappy woman backward and forward on her bed with great violence. And in Finland, mothers were encouraged to force babies out by jumping down from heights of four to ten feet. One can only imagine "the ruptures of the uterus, tears of the birth canal, and hemorrhages"[45] that attended this kind of violent intervention.

If all this shaking and jumping failed to induce birth, the next step would be for the local midwife to try to pull out the child by any part she could get hold of. If the child's arm was the presenting part (a transverse lie), tugging would be particularly disastrous. Today, a transverse lie would be dealt with by a caesarean section, and even in the eighteenth century a well-informed doctor would push the baby's arm back into the uterus in hope that the situation would correct itself naturally (and in a small percentage of cases it did). But for a village midwife in premodern Europe, a standard course of action was to pull mightily on the arm, hoping thus to pull out the child—a feat that was anatomically impossible. Or she might cut off the arm and wait to see what might happen next. But tugging and butchering were useless, they just intensified the laboring woman's torment, the wretched result was always the same: The child's torso remained behind in the mother, and the undelivered mother died an unspeakable, agonized death.

According to Shorter, prior to the nineteenth century, the village midwives of Europe and North America often wreaked havoc. Constantly pulling and hauling at the mother's birth canal, at the infant's head, and at the placenta, "they were captives of a folkloric view that the best midwife is the one who interferes most." When a midwife arrived on the scene she might first "break the waters"—puncturing the amniotic sac with a dirty fingernail or sharp instrument. In the 1920s an elderly Swiss midwife proudly showed a visiting doctor a thimble with a jagged top that she used to puncture the sac. And as late as the 1940s, midwives in the Valais still used goose grease to lubricate both their hands and the private parts of the mother.

All of this interference dramatically increased the likelihood of infection. No wonder that postdelivery sepsis—the modern term for "childbed fever"—was a source of universal anxiety to women giving birth. According to Shorter, up until the nineteenth century, 1 in 20 of all deliveries triggered a life-threatening infection in the mother.

But even if a woman passed through childbirth safely, she was not out of the woods. If she had experienced a brutal, long, drawn-out delivery, the odds were that she would be maimed for life. Shorter describes how various kinds of "fistulas"—openings between the vagina and neighboring organs—could render a

woman incontinent for the rest of her life. According to
J. F. Dieffenbach, a German surgeon who practiced in
the 1830s:

> A sadder situation can hardly exist than that of
> a woman afflicted with a fistula. A source of dis-
> gust, even to herself, the woman beloved by her
> husband becomes, in this condition, the object of
> bodily revulsion to him. The labia, perineum,
> lower part of the buttocks and thighs and calves
> are continually wet. The refreshment of a change
> of clothing provides no relief because the clean
> undergarment, after being quickly saturated, slaps
> against the patients, flopping against their wet
> thighs as they walk, sloshing in their wet shoes as
> though they were wading through a swamp.
>
> The bed does not soothe them, because a good
> resting place, a bed, or a horsehair mattress, is
> quickly impregnated with urine and gives off the
> most unbearable stench. Even the richest are usu-
> ally condemned for life to a straw sack, whose
> straw must be renewed daily.[46]

By the mid-nineteenth century, fistulas could be dealt
with by a surgical procedure, but this did not end the
mutilation of mothers. Forceps had just become fashionable, and their widespread use—and abuse—by ill-
trained doctors led to much more tearing of the
reproductive organs. According to some scholars, cer-

tain kinds of gynecological damage actually increased in the second half of the nineteenth century. Dr. W. J. Sinclair, in an address to the Annual Meeting of the British Medical Association in 1897, had harsh words for doctors. According to Sinclair, a forceps delivery had become "the bloodiest operation in medical practice," because doctors were in an unseemly rush deliver the child. "It is by no means a rare thing to find a young woman suffering from dislocation of the uterus and lacerations of the cervix and of the perineum, whose first labour was terminated by forceps a mere four to six hours after the onset of regular pains." Sinclair estimated that the percentage of forceps delivery resulting in injury to the mother was as high as 85 percent in some hospitals.[47]

Among poor women, perineum tears were commonly not repaired, and if the tear involved the anus, the woman would suffer fecal incontinence for the rest of her life. In the 1920s, activist physician Maria Stopes saw thousands of working-class women in her London clinic and was incensed by the uncaring, supercilious attitude of doctors. "They come away after a serious and painful delivery," she said, "leaving the mother with a lacerated cervix and a torn perineum. More often than not, they make no attempt at an operation to right these injuries." Stopes tells of women patients who continued to be racked by pelvic and back pain—twenty years after a botched delivery.[48]

If ignorant midwives and unfeeling doctors produced gratuitous torture, so did misogynist religious practices. For several centuries in premodern France and Germany, Catholic priests refused to bury in consecrated ground a woman who died in childbirth. Instead she was buried outside the churchyard along with the suicides. According to Catholic doctrine, blood, shed during childbirth (lochia) was thought to be particularly "polluting" and a new mother needed to be officially "churched"—a ceremony that took place a month after birth—before being readmitted into the religious community.[49] Thus, a woman dying in childbirth was not entitled to receive the sacraments and her final hours were bereft of religious comfort or consolation.

When I first read *Women's Bodies,* I was filled with fury. I was furious at village midwives who infected new mothers and inflicted such gratuitous agony. I was furious at celibate priests hell-bent on punishing dying mothers for their carnal sins by refusing to comfort or bury them. I was even furious at conventions of modesty and prudery that prevented women from seeking help for their terrible injuries. Anything that compounded the torture of pain-wracked, laboring women was grist to my mill. Yet when my fury abated, I was left with a perspective on childbirth that was both more nuanced and more humble.

I found myself more fully aware of just how thor-

oughly babies and birthing have limited women's lives.
No wonder premodern women accomplished so little in
the wider world! Simply negotiating everyday life
when you have no bladder function and have just
buried a two-year-old is a major challenge. If a woman
bore enough children, she didn't need patriarchy to
keep her down!

I found myself newly appreciative of the enormous
privilege wrapped up in being a woman at this time, in
this place. At the beginning of the twenty-first century,
American women have a huge measure of control over
their own fertility. If they decide to become pregnant,
they can look forward to the delivery of a healthy
child; and count on childbirth being a risk-free, even
pleasurable experience. This constellation of extraordinary freedoms is only 30 years old.

I also found myself newly concerned that women not
squander their brand-new freedoms. If women no
longer need to fear their fertility, they surely need to
respect it. A woman's window of fertility remains
extraordinarily short. As we have discovered in this
chapter, a woman still needs to deal with childbirth in
a timely fashion if she is to count on being able to
enjoy risk-free pregnancies and joyous births. Just
remember: Our foremothers would have given their
eyeteeth for such choices.

PART II

SOLUTIONS

6

THE TIME CRUNCH

*I*N FEBRUARY 2001, I CONDUCTED an informal focus group with eight young professionals who worked at three firms in Cambridge, Massachusetts—an Internet consulting firm, a venture capital firm, and an advertising agency. The session was held in the offices of Global IT Strategies, where three of the young people worked. Just down the road from MIT, this small firm has a fast-growing list of blue-chip clients and has attracted some of the best talent in the Boston area. Predator territory, I thought as I walked in.

The offices of Global IT Strategies were predictably edgy and hip: winter sunshine bouncing off stark,

white walls, understated beechwood desks, amber and
lime green chairs. No clunky furniture or shag rugs
here. The whole place smacked of youthful energy.

We holed up in the conference room for an entire
morning, myself along with six women and two men,
who ranged in age from 26 to 34. Glamorous, smart,
sharp, and irreverent, they came from all over—
Boston, Australia, England, California, and Texas—
and all held demanding, fast-track jobs. One was
married, one was living with a partner, the others were
single. None had children, although five of the women
spoke wistfully about children being a short-term goal.

Much of the discussion centered on time—or the
lack of it. It reverberated throughout the conversation
like a drumbeat:

Jennifer: This career of mine is eating me alive. I
mean, it's stimulating and challenging and I love
working for this particular firm, but the time
demands are awesome.

When I'm working in Cambridge it's not too
bad. I get in at about 8:30 A.M. and leave at 7.30
P.M. Now I do check my e-mail twice during the
course of an evening, but we're still talking about
a pretty decent workweek—fifty-eight hours or so.
It's when I'm working with a client at a project
site that the hours get insane. Since I'm on the
road four days a week for two-thirds of the year,
this is a big chunk of my reality.

On the road, here's what happens: I work at the client's office from 8:00 A.M. to 7:00 P.M., I then have a team meeting over dinner—to coordinate, and strategize—and then, at around 9:30 P.M. I go back to my hotel room and check my e-mail to see what else I have to do.

Paula: Don't forget voice mail. We all have voice mail at the office and voice mail on our cell phones, both of which we check on a daily basis. Between e-mail and voice mail you can count on an additional three items of work at the end of the day. So at 10 P.M., there you are in your hotel room, working on your laptop, responding to a question from some other client.

Annabel: and the phone rings and it's the new boyfriend back in Boston who's fuming because he's been calling all evening and hasn't been able to reach you. You try explaining that you've just finished a two-and-a-half-hour team dinner with colleagues (yes, some of these colleagues are male), and although you sound a little tipsy (yes, I did have wine with dinner), you actually have to get back to work. And by the way, you'll be back Friday, but won't have much time this weekend because you need to leave Sunday evening for a four-day trip to Albuquerque (yes, this is a business trip).

Rachel: It's hard on boyfriends. I had a date with this guy last month. At the end of the evening he said, "When can I see you? How about next week?" I said, "I'm sorry, but I'm going to be out of town working on a new account." And he said, "Well, how about the following week?" And I said, "You're not going to believe this, but I won't know my travel schedule until closer to the time, I can't make any plans yet." At that point he threw up his hands and, in an annoyed tone of voice, said, "How d'you expect a relationship to get off the ground?"

Dan: It's just hard on relationships period. I moved in with my girlfriend a year ago and we're really trying to make it work. But two weeks of every month I'm not even in the country. My company is very active in Eastern Europe, which means that each month I have an extended business trip to either Prague or Warsaw. She just gets very lonely. I mean, it's not that we spend a lot of time together when I'm in town—she's in real estate and works very long hours, too—but at least we have dinner together. There's this precious time between 9:00 P.M. and 10:30 P.M. that we can plan on spending together.

Natalie: You know, I really love my work. It's draining and demanding, but it's also exhilarating. You get to work with an extraordinary range of clients and issues. In my book, there's no better feeling than sinking your teeth into a complex, multilayered problem and solving it.

But I don't know whether I can survive in this business over the long haul. This is the third consulting firm I've worked for, and I've yet to see an older, more senior woman whose life I would actually want.

Rachel, clearly shocked: What do you mean?

Natalie: I know a few hard-driving women who are climbing the ladder at consulting firms, but they are single—or divorced—and seem pretty isolated. And I know a handful of working mothers who are trying to do the half-time thing or the two-thirds time thing. They work reduced hours so they can see their kids, but they don't get the good projects, they don't get the bonuses, and they also get whispered about behind their backs. You know, comments like: If she's not prepared to work the client's hours, she has no business being in the profession.

Sonia: I hear those same whispers and, quite frankly, they scare me. I just turned 28 and have been married a year. I'm terrified of having children. To me it's synonymous with waving good-bye to being taken seriously, waving good-bye to first-class citizenship.

Annabel: It's not true elsewhere. I've worked for
European companies where professionals who opt
for a reduced workweek are not marginalized. I
mean, they're used on the high-profile projects
and treated with respect. But in the U.S. it's different. Here, the 'inside team' is made up of the
people who bump into each other in the hallway
at 11 o'clock at night. But how does a woman
with children work until 11:00 P.M. on a regular
basis?

Sonia: At my last job, part-timers got stigmatized
so badly that I often thought they might as well be
walking around with a scarlet letter emblazoned
on their chests.

But I don't think it had a whole lot to do with
performance or efficiency. I see no reason why a
professional at an advertising agency can't go half
time and deal with half as many clients. In my
view, what it really comes down to is attitudes and
mind-sets.

Colleagues are simply jealous. Advertising is a
profession that creates a famine on the time front.
Therefore anyone who gets a break is seen as
avoiding paying his or her dues and is resented: If
you take a two-thirds or a four-fifths workweek,
you can expect to take a lot of heat—to be
punished in some way. The only way around this
is for everyone to get a better deal. I mean, why

should anyone have to work a seventy-hour week?

Jeff: I'll second that. One thing that gets me riled up is the assumption that the only people entitled to a life outside of work are women with children. But how does a man become a halfway decent partner if he has to work every waking hour?

Rachel: That's a good point. But I guess at least you guys aren't dealing with a biological clock and have the option of having children later in life when you're more established.

I used to be so critical of women who got married and had their children young. It seemed so wrongheaded—raising kids on very little money before you've seen the world or worked out your own identity. But now I think they may have been on to something. At least they have their children.

When I look into the future I don't know how I'm going to do it all. I'm twenty-nine now and know I need to go back to school and get an MBA. After that there will be a big push to take my career to the next level. And yet these are also the years I would like to get married and have children. How do I reconcile these goals? I haven't a clue.

Jennifer: Part of my problem is that I come from this picture-book family. My mom ran a beautiful

home and looked after my dad, but she also proof-
read my history papers and drove me to swim
team practice at 7:00 A.M. Saturday morning. I
once added it up: She spent seventeen hours a
week supporting me in a variety of activities. If
I have a family, I'm going to be faced with those
impossible standards.

Paula: Time is just a huge issue. You just can't get
around it. Expectations are so high. We have these
high-powered careers that sit in the center
of our lives. But we also want an emotionally
nourishing relationship with a man—someone
who's not just a stuffed shirt. Relationships take
time. No two ways around it. And a little ways
down the road we also want a child or two.
Children we fully intend to spend all kinds of
quality time with.

From where I sit, it doesn't seem possible to do
all three things—they just won't fit into a life, at
least not simultaneously.[1]

This free-floating anxiety about time—how to get
enough of it, how to gain control over it—reverberates
far beyond the walls of one conference room. As we discovered in *High-Achieving Women, 2001,* women are
dealing with long and lengthening workweeks in a
great many sectors and occupations. Twenty-nine percent of high achievers and 34 percent of ultra-achiev-

ers are at work more than 50 hours a week, and a significant proportion of these women are on the job 10–20 more hours a week than they were five years ago. Few of these women can count on much help from their spouse or partner. Whether it's doing the laundry or driving the children to Little League practice, only a small percentage of husbands (3–12 percent) take prime responsibility for house-related or child-related tasks.

These high-achieving women tend to look to their workplaces for relief. And at least some of them are finding it. Barbara, 45, is a part-time partner at a Boston law firm.[2] She works four days a week and could not be more pleased with her schedule:

> I thank my lucky stars that I came up for partnership in a progressive firm that gave me the chance to prove I could make a reduced schedule work over the long haul. And I've produced! My clients are happy, and I've pulled in new business.
>
> My salary is obviously lower than it would be if I worked full-time, but for me that's an easy trade-off. I have two children, ages nine and twelve, and I have turned Fridays into this magical day where I catch up with myself and do special projects with them. Sure, I stay in touch with the office—I take my Blackberry everywhere—but last Friday Sophie and I planted a garden

after school, and this Friday I'm taking Jonathan
to the Science Museum.

According to *High-Achieving Women, 2001*, some
employers do provide significant time relief: 12 percent
offer job-protected leave and 31 percent offer job sharing. Many more, however, offer only time flexibility: 69
percent offer staggered hours and 48 percent offer
work-at-home options. These less ambitious policies
seem to be of limited use to time-pressed, high-achieving women.

For the last five years Joanna, 39, has worked as an
account executive at a head-hunting firm in Chicago.
She always thought her firm had great work/life policies—until she adopted a child:

> I don't mean to sound ungrateful, but this com-
> pany has a whole slew of benefits—flextime,
> telecommuting, emergency childcare, and
> concierge services—but they don't add up to a
> whole lot. In my opinion they're chicken feed.
>
> My main problem—the one that keeps me
> awake at night—is the number of hours I am
> expected to put in. I work sixty hours a week fifty
> weeks of the year, which leaves precious little time
> for anything else. How am I supposed to bond
> with my baby if I don't finish my last assignment
> until after she goes to bed at night? Telecom-

muting and emergency childcare don't give me time with my child.

What I crave is a reduced schedule—three-fifths time sounds good. I know this should cost me, and I'm prepared to take a salary cut, but it's no go. I asked my boss and was told that the firm doesn't want to establish a precedent. I almost told him that "maybe this is a precedent worth establishing," but I stopped myself. I hit the job market last month and don't want to tell my colleagues yet. I'm out there looking for either a part-time job or a job-share. So far I've gotten two nibbles. We'll see.

The working mothers I interviewed as a follow-up to *High-Achieving Women, 2001* were clear on one point, conventional benefits packages which are limited to such items as flextime, telecommuting, and childcare assistance, simply don't do enough to rein in the workday and work year. According to these women, the long-hours culture has become so oppressive that tinkering around at the margins no longer does the trick—at least not if you are interested in having a family. A delayed start Monday morning, permission to telecommute Friday morning, or even the ability to put baby Lucy in the company nursery, just don't cut the mustard in a world where the "normal" workload—week in and week out—is 50 or 60 hours and the "normal" vacation is 11 days a year. The kind of relationships high-achieving women are interested in—with significant others, with children—require something more substantial than the energy left over after a 13-hour day.

Think of what a 55-hour week means in terms of work/life balance. Assuming an hour lunch and a 45-minute round-trip commute (the national average), the workday stretches to almost 13 hours: 7:30 A.M. to 8:15 P.M., or 8:30 A.M. to 9:15 P.M. Even without "extras" (out-of-town trips, client dinners, power breakfasts), this kind of schedule makes it extremely difficult for a professional to jump-start a relationship or to be a "good enough" parent. A mother of a five or eight-year-old who works a 55-hour week would not make it home in time to eat dinner with her child, and would only have a fighting chance of getting home in time to read a bedtime story and kiss her child good night. The working mothers who participated in the survey made it abundantly clear that what they want most are work/life policies that confer on them what one woman called "the gift of time."

Amy, 41, works as a marketing executive at an IBM facility in Austin, Texas. Her son, Kevin, just turned three and Amy is newly back at work:

> People don't believe me when I tell them that my
> company offers a three-year personal leave of

absence. Some people take it to look after a child
or an elderly parent; others take it to go back to
school. Now this leave is unpaid, so you do need to
have an employed spouse, but the company provides benefits and job-back guarantees.

I can't tell you how grateful I am to have had
this kind of time out. Because of infertility problems, it took us five years to conceive Kevin and
he is likely to be our only child, so I was particularly eager to savor his babyhood. I breastfed him
until he was eighteen months old, signed us both
up for 'music together,' and made friends in the
neighborhood. Most of all, I avoided splitting
myself in two. I know so many new mothers who
are tugged and pulled in all directions when they
go back to work too soon.

This three-year leave enabled Kevin and me to
establish a bond so strong that I feel we can with-
stand anything that comes down the pike. IBM
gave me this gift and I will always be grateful.

The women who participated in *High-Achieving
Women, 2001*—Barbara, Joanna, and Amy among
them—were asked to consider a list of policy options
that would help them achieve balance in their lives
over the long haul. Overwhelmingly they endorsed the
following cluster of work/life policies that would make
it much easier to get off conventional career ladders
and eventually get back on. (Note: The first figures rep-

resent high-achieving career women; the figures in parentheses represent high-potential women currently not in careers; see definition in chapter 2.)

A Time Bank of Paid Parenting Leave

88 percent (86 percent) of respondents support the creation of a time bank to allow for three months of paid parenting leave, which can be taken throughout a child's life up until he or she is 18 years old.

Restructured Retirement Plans

87 percent (91 percent) of respondents would like retirement plans to be restructured so as to eliminate the penalty for career interruptions.

Career Breaks

85 percent (87 percent) of respondents would like the option of taking an official "career break," which could consist of up to three years of unpaid, job-protected leave.

Reduced-Hour Careers

85 percent (91 percent) of respondents support the creation of part-time career tracks—high-level jobs that allow for reduced hours and a reduced workload on an ongoing basis, but also allow for the possibility of promotion.

Separated Part-Time Job Listings

85 percent (90 percent) of respondents would like job listings for part-time or flexible schedule positions to be listed separately in newspapers, trade publications, and websites.

Tax Breaks for Reentry

81 percent (88 percent) of respondents would like to see tax breaks or subsidies for reentry programs that enable professionals to get back up to speed before returning to the workforce.

Alumni Status

74 percent (79 percent) of respondents would welcome the creation of "alumni status" for former employees. Alumni would continue to provide certain kinds of advice and guidance, and where applicable, the company would continue to pay their dues and certification fees so they could maintain professional standing. Analogous to active retirement, alumni status would help professional women who have left careers stay "in the loop."

What does this wish list tell us?

Whether they are 28 or 55, whether they are currently in careers or currently at home, high-achieving women understand that a worsening time famine is at the heart of their struggle to lead more balanced lives and they would like employers and government to be much more creative in designing work/life policies that provide the "gift of time." By huge margins (eight or nine to one) these women want imaginative versions of paid and unpaid leave as well as part-time career options. They also want institutional changes, which range from rethinking the way jobs are listed to pension plan reform.

All of which brings us to a critical question: How realistic is this wish list?

Are companies anywhere close to instituting the policies women want? If not, what might induce them? Before answering these questions we need to back up and provide a little historical perspective.

Concern about the time crunch has been with us for more than a decade. In the nineties, books such as *The Overworked American* by Juliet Schor and *The Time Bind* by Arlie Hochschild contended that Americans were working more hours—per week and per year— than at any time since the Second World War.[3] Subsequent studies have refined the analysis.[4] It seems that workweeks have not expanded across the board, rather, there is a growing bifurcation in working hours, with a large increase in the number of workers who work long hours (50 hours or more a week), coexisting with a large increase in the number who work part time (30 hours or less a week).[5] These sharply divergent trends are linked to education and occupation. Short and shrinking workweeks are typical of jobs requiring less education and tend to be at the low end of the labor market. Long and lengthening workweeks—a central concern of this book—are typical of managerial jobs requiring college degrees and tend to be at the high end of the labor market. As we know from the data contained in *High-Achieving Women, 2001,* some of the more dramatic trends concern women. Indeed, according to sociologists Jerry Jacobs and Kathleen Gerson, "The percentage of women working fifty hours per week or more is now higher in America than in any other country in the world."[6]

Why do so many professionals—women and men—feel constrained to work longer and longer hours? Several structural and cultural factors contribute directly to the ever-expanding American workweek.

In most companies, senior management is under intense pressure to use its professional workforce for as many hours a week as possible. This is because there are no marginal costs attached to high-echelon workers. The reasons for this go back to 1938 when Congress passed the Fair Labor Standards Act, which institutionalized the 40-hour week and required employers to pay overtime for any additional hours worked. One provision, however, exempted managers and professionals. This might not have produced overload back in 1938, when only 15 percent of employees were in the exempt category, and most of these were men with stay-at-home wives. But it produces significant overload in 2001 when close to 30 percent of employees are in the exempt category and many of them are parents who do not have an at-home partner.

The reality is when managers and professionals do not qualify for extra pay for additional hours spent on the job, the marginal cost of labor falls to zero—a fact that undoubtedly encourages long workweeks. In this circumstance, employers have a strong incentive to squeeze as many hours as possible out of professional employees because this reduces unit labor costs. Professionals fall in line because employers use "number of hours worked" as the basis for promotion and future compensation.

The size and structure of benefits packages also contribute to longer workweeks. The cost of providing employment benefits such as health insurance and pensions has climbed steadily in recent years and now makes up about 25 percent of an employee's total compensation. Since the cost of most benefits is fixed for a full-time employee, no matter how many hours he or she works, the real hourly cost of such benefits declines as a professional spends more hours on the job. So again, an employer has a strong incentive to wring as many hours as possible out of professional employees.[7]

Now obviously there's a limit to how hard an employer can press and squeeze. At some point, a professional employee—most likely a woman with family responsibilities—will refuse to deal with a workweek that has expanded to 50 or 60 hours and will either quit completely or go to work for another company with more options on the work/life front. This kind of "professional flight" becomes much more likely when labor markets are tight and highly skilled employees can pick and choose between alternative job possibilities. All of which spells trouble for employers. Professional flight can be hugely expensive for companies because of the stiff costs attached to labor turnover.

The fact of the matter is, losing skilled personnel is enormously expensive. There are the direct costs of finding a replacement—advertising charges, headhunter fees, and the "opportunity cost" of time spent selecting and interviewing candidates. There are also significant indirect costs—the defector's lost leads and contacts, the new employee's depressed productivity while getting "up to speed," and the time coworkers spend guiding and training.

A 2001 study by the American Society for Training and Development estimated that when all factors are considered, the cost of replacing a typical professional is approximately one and a half times the departing person's yearly salary.[8] A study by the Work-Family

Task Force at the University of Texas came to a similar estimate of 93 percent to 200 percent of the departing employee's salary.[9] The rule of thumb seems to be, the more senior the person, the higher the cost of replacing him or her. According to Anne Ruddy, executive director of WorldatWork, a global network of human resource professionals, the bill for filling the slot of a high-level executive is about three times the job's annual salary.[10]

Turnover costs tend to be particularly high in "hot" sectors of the labor market during times of rapid economic growth. In the late 1990s Integral Training Systems Search Inc., a national consulting and training firm, estimated the cost of replacing a single software engineer at $150,000–$200,000.[11] An October, 2000 survey by the American Management Association reported that 76 percent of human resource managers were finding it more expensive to recruit high-echelon workers than it had been three or five years earlier.[12]

In recent months the economy has clearly slowed down, but corporate executives continue to talk convincingly about the costs associated with failing to retain talented professionals. According to Paul Sacks, CEO of Multinational Strategies, a New York–based management consulting firm, "losing a valued professional is extremely expensive. It undermines relationships with clients and jeopardizes the work of an entire work team. In my business it behooves you to ride out a period of slow growth without shedding key personnel."[13] A recent article in the *Harvard Business Review* makes the same point. During a downturn smart executives don't panic and shed employees. The average recession lasts only eleven months, so why scramble to fire—and then rehire and retrain? In the modern world such a response is inefficient because it is newly difficult—and hugely expensive—to recruit talented people.[14]

Thus, despite the downturn, a sizable number of companies seem willing to stay the course and continue to develop work/life policies that both attract and retain highly skilled women. Lisa Benenson, former editor in chief of *Working Mother* and *Working Woman* magazines, points to the fact that *Working Mother* has a growing pool of companies to choose from when the magazine compiles its annual list of the best companies to work for.[15] Indeed, a recent survey of 1,000 large companies found that 87 percent provided childcare assistance, up from 78 percent in 1993, while 77 percent provided flextime, up from 60 percent in 1993. A few offer elaborate work/life policy packages. See in particular the top ten companies selected by *Working Woman* in the magazine's annual survey of the "100 Best Companies for Working

Mothers." In 2000 the top ten included such companies as Allstate Insurance Company, Bank of America, and Eli Lilly and Company.[16] Ernst & Young, IBM, Merck, and Scholastic do particularly well on the time-enhancement front. These companies go some considerable distance toward giving their employees the gift of time.[17]

High-Achieving Women, 2001 provides concrete proof that companies offering a rich array of work/life policies are much more likely to hang on to their professional women than companies that don't. According to the survey, women who stay in their careers tend to work for companies that offer substantial help on the work/life front. Between 42 and 69 percent of these women have access to flextime, telecommuting, paid parenting leave and compressed workweeks. In contrast, women who left careers tended to work for companies that had less-well-developed work/life policies. Only 28 to 49 percent of these high-potential women worked for companies that had this same range of benefits (see chart in notes).[18]

But it's not just better benefits packages women need, it's also the ability to use them. High-achieving women who stayed in careers felt strongly that not only did their companies offer generous policies, but that their managers were supportive of the use of these policies—indeed, almost 90 percent said they had made personal use of at least one. Again, women who had left felt differently. These women reported that at their last job, managers had not been supportive of work/life policies even if they were in place.

Companies these days seem buffeted by two competing imperatives: the need to minimize labor costs by squeezing professional employees so that they spend as many hours as possible on the job, and the need to minimize turnover costs by implementing work/life policies that reduce hours spent on the job. In most workplaces, these imperatives clash and collide, which is why employees often feel there are two sets of rules: one written and official, the other unwritten and unofficial.

The official rules are those laid out in company handbooks and manuals that technically define the conditions of employment. They tend to highlight recently established work/life policies. The unofficial rules are unwritten, but are embedded in the corporate culture and need to be taken extremely seriously by any employee wanting to be tapped for promotion. These rules emphasize the need to put in all kinds of face time—12–14 hour days in the office very visibly "on the job." As sociologist and Philadelphia-based family activist Jessica DeGroot explains, the more face time an employee puts in, the more points he or she gets, but some face time is more valuable than other face time: "The face time ritual deducts points for the woman who comes in at 7:00 A.M. so she can pick up her child at the daycare center by 6:00 P.M. It adds points for the man who comes in at 9:00 A.M. and stays at his desk until 8:00 P.M. This is because 'after hours' face time yields the highest points of all."[19]

The fact is, the pressures to cut costs by squeezing professionals have been with us a long time, much longer than the pressure to cut costs by lowering turnover rates. Over the last several decades, corporate America has developed an extremely unforgiving long-hour culture that is hard to shake, even in the face of compelling evidence showing that reducing employee turnover may be a better way to cut costs in the long run. In the words of Jacobs and Gerson, "Long workweeks persist—and spread—not because they are, necessarily, the most efficient way of organizing work, but because a long-hours culture has succeeded in 'stigmatizing' those who work less."[20] As the participants in my young professionals focus group pointed out, refusing to work long hours can brand a professional employee with the modern-day equivalent of a scarlet letter. Such a person is seen as a "deviant" or an "outcast," unworthy of serious consideration for advancement.

It takes an extremely gutsy professional to ignore the unwritten, unofficial rulebook, break rank, and actually take at face value what is written in the official rule book. In fact, it is so difficult that professionals are starting to reach out for help.

Ellen Ostrow, Ph.D., is a new breed of psychologist. Founder of LawyersLifeCoach.com, a website that provides resources to help lawyers combat the long-hours trend, she provides personal and career coaching for lawyers determined to achieve balance: to work shorter hours and get themselves a life. Specifically she seeks to help young attorneys—most often women, but sometimes men—buck brutal requirements for billable hours and 70-hour to 80-hour-workweeks, and actually take advantage of the work/life policies newly on the books. On her website Ostrow describes the struggle of one seventh-year associate at a large law firm who was making a valiant effort to both be successful in her career and stay involved in her children's lives:

> There seemed to be little doubt that she would make partner. But she had reached the end of her rope just as she was about to grasp the golden ring. She'd been working a reduced hour schedule for several years. Reduced hours meant she could leave in time to meet her children when they came home from school.
>
> However, to get her work done, she had to go back to work after the children went to sleep. So for months she'd been working from 9:00 P.M. until 1:00 or 2:00 in the morning . . . But exhaustion was far less a problem for her than her isola-

tion at the firm. She felt like a pariah or a disabled
person. Although her firm allowed part-time
schedules, she felt they were regarded as a special
accommodation to the family-challenged; for people ostensibly not tough enough to do everything.

"I speak to a lot of part-time attorneys who are debili-
tated by guilt," says Ostrow.[21]

One thing seems clear. Having a raft of work/life
policies on the books is one thing, changing the culture
of the firm so that these policies are freely available to
individual professionals is something else entirely.

So where do we go from here? Can we craft policies—in workplaces and in government—that succeed
on both the official and unofficial fronts? Can we for-
malize a policy package that both creates the possibility of work/life balance, and changes mind-sets and
attitudes so that our long-hours culture can be transformed?

I believe we can and have come up with a list of policy options that I hope will be a start for both individuals and government. Paying prime attention to the
needs and desires of women, and factoring in what I
have learned to be the real-world constraints of
employers, I have crafted a small package of policies
that reflect "the art of the possible." Don't get me
wrong. This package will not produce utopia. But it is
capable of making a great deal of difference to

women's ability to balance their lives. Even more important, it is realistic and doable. Here's what I advocate:

A Work/Life Policy Package

PRIVATE SECTOR INITIATIVES

1. Give every working parent a time bank of six months of paid leave, portions of which can be taken throughout a child's life until he or she is 18 years old.

As any mom or dad knows, the demands of a newborn are urgent, but not unique. A child can be extremely needy at any age. If a child flunks fourth grade or plunges into depression at puberty, a parent may well want to take some time off work—to find the right help, or to be more available.

Spreading paid parenting leave over 18 years has the additional benefit of undercutting discrimination. Once it is clear that paid parenting leave can be taken by both men and women at any time over an 18-year time span, discrimination against married women in the childbearing years becomes much less likely. It is also true that when paid parenting leave is flexible and generous, sexual stereotypes begin to break down. The Swedish model is relevant here. In 1974, when parenting leave was first introduced in Sweden, only 3 percent of fathers took advantage of it. By the late 1990s, 80 percent of fathers were taking at least part of this leave.

2. Create high-level jobs that allow for reduced hours and a reduced workload on an ongoing basis.

The challenge here is to ensure that these reduced-hour jobs are not dead ends, but allow for the possibility of promotion, while bearing in mind that it will take longer to accumulate the necessary experience. As we have seen, various professional service firms are experimenting with part-time partnerships. Flexibility seems to be the key here. Even with a reduced client load, a part-time professional needs to bend with the needs of clients.

It's paradoxical to realize that this proposal is a gender-neutral version of Felice Schwartz's infamous "Mommy Track."[22] The suggestion she made 12 years ago that professional women might need reduced-hour careers provoked a storm of opposition. Feminists, trade unionists, and other progressives were appalled at an idea that they saw as "trying to shunt female employees off on a slow road to nowhere."[23] A galloping time crunch has made her proposal much more acceptable today.

It's worth noting that in Europe professionals have access to a variety of reduced-hour options. In Sweden, mothers and fathers are entitled to limit their workday to six hours until a child is eight years old. In the Netherlands the official workweek is 36 hours, and in France the workweek has recently been reduced to 35 hours. Indeed, Europeans now work a staggering 350 fewer hours a year than Americans do, and the gap is particularly wide for professional employees.[24]

3. Develop "off-ramps" and "on-ramps."

For many overworked professionals, achieving work/life balance means interrupting conventional career trajectories. As we discovered in chapter 3, such interruptions come at a high price—in terms of both earnings and promotion—because it's relatively easy to leave a career, but very difficult to restart one. Policy analyst Nancy Rankin compares careers to highways, and makes the point that we need to develop at least as many "on-ramps" as "off-ramps."[25] In this regard, the following options would be helpful: *Career breaks,* which would allow employees to take unpaid, job-protected leave and return to work. *Alumni status,* which would allow employees to preserve ties to their companies and professions. *Separate job listings,* which would make reduced-hour jobs easier to find. And *alternative retirement plans,* which would reduce the long-term penalties attached to taking time out.

GOVERNMENT INITIATIVES

1. Extend the Family Medical Leave Act (FMLA) to workers in small companies and turn it into paid leave.

As explained in chapter 3, FMLA has been available since 1993 and provides 12 weeks of job protected leave for the purpose of looking after a new child—or an elderly parent or seriously ill family member. This legislation is of central importance to women. As we have seen, job-protected parenting leave not only allows a working mother to take time to bond with a newborn, it permits her to avoid career interruptions and thus maintain her earning power. At the moment, FMLA is unpaid and limited to workers in companies with more than 50 employees. We need to turn it into paid leave and make it universally available.[26]

2. Provide tax incentives to companies that offer employees "the gift of time."

The list of eligible benefits should include: reduced-hour jobs, job sharing, paid parenting leave, telecommuting, and compressed workweeks. Under the terms of this program a company would qualify for a tax break by offering employees at least three of these time-enhancing benefits.

3. Promote new legislation to eliminate incentives for long-hour weeks.

The goal here is to remove the perverse incentives that lie behind our long-hours culture. Reducing the percentage of employees who are exempt from overtime and adopting a benefits plan that would peg benefits to number of hours worked are both measures that would increase the marginal cost of professional labor and therefore force employers to keep long workweeks to a minimum. To make this a reality, government should *extend the Fair Labor Standards Act* to many more professional and managerial employees so that they become eligible for overtime. Government should also *require mandatory benefits that accrue in proportion to number of hours worked*. This would entitle workers who work very long hours to receive additional benefits (retirement contributions, life insurance, or cash bonuses), and would protect part-time workers.

The policy package described above embodies some powerful principles:

First and foremost it reflects the needs and desires of professional women who, in overwhelming numbers, want work/life options that give them the gift of time. This package is therefore a departure from conventional work/life packages, which all too often focus on measures that enhance work rather than on those that enhance time. Sick-child care is an example of a benefit that reduces the impediments to work by off-loading a needy child and making sure that a mother or father can continue working. But even if the needs of a child are being well attended to, a parent may well prefer to be home with a sick son or daughter.

Reduced-hour jobs, paid parenting leave, telecommuting—this is the kind of package that allows an individual to shift the boundary between work and family and achieve long-term balance. These options might even allow a professional couple to contemplate what child psychologist Stanley Greenspan calls "the four-thirds solution"—an arrangement whereby each partner allocates two-thirds time to career and one-third time to family, and together they provide four-thirds of a single income.[27] Greenspan describes this solution as "an optimal framework" for child development and adult well-being.

Secondly, these policies recognize the fact that America's long-hours culture must be tackled head-on by removing the perverse incentives that lead to 50- and 60-hour workweeks. If employers were hit with overtime and fringe-benefit charges every time they squeezed an extra five or ten hours out of a professional employee, they might think twice about requiring long workweeks. Most probably the top stratum of senior managers should remain exempt from overtime—CEOs, for example, who are almost always rewarded with year-end bonuses, should not expect to work 40 hours a week or be paid overtime—but fully 30 percent of all employees are now in the exempt category, and many would be better served if they were eligible for overtime pay.

Thirdly, if implemented, this policy package would be enormously constructive on the gender-equity front. Curbing our long-hours culture will help to level the playing field between men and women. As long as large numbers of professional workers continue to put in 50, 60, even 70 hours a week, individuals who choose to take advantage of extended leave or reduced-hour workweeks will pay an extremely high price in terms of career advancement and earning power. And mothers will pay this price disproportionately.

This is not only because mothers are more motivated than fathers to spend time with their children, it is also because professional women tend to earn less than their husbands and this creates an incentive for mom rather than dad to take time off work. Together, these factors combine to create a debilitating circle: Lower earnings increases the likelihood of career interruptions for mothers, which, in turn, leads to even lower earnings down the road.

Thus, reining in our long-hours culture is central to

promoting gender equity. Once we have narrowed the definition of what constitutes "exempt" labor, few professionals would work long workweeks, there would be much-reduced penalties attached to taking time out, and hopefully, many more men would feel free to do so. In such a world, many more couples might choose Greenspan's four-thirds solution and both men and women would have a better shot at balanced lives.

Finally, these policies would go some distance toward healing what is becoming an ugly rift in workplaces around the country: between parents and the childfree. In *High-Achieving Women, 2001,* fully 54 percent of childless career women say that people without children are unfairly expected to pick up the slack for those who have children; indeed, 45 percent of these women say that people with children have altogether too many options or benefits.

Anna, 52, is managing editor of a publishing company based in San Francisco and participated in the survey:

> If anyone else walks into my office and tells me
> she's pregnant I will have a hard time being
> polite, let alone congratulatory. I have eleven
> women on my staff and two are expecting in the
> fall, which means they will be out for our busiest
> season, leaving the rest of us to do their work. One

of the women had the gall to ask for some additional unpaid leave. She told me six weeks wasn't
long enough. I don't know whether that's true or
not—I've never had children. But I don't believe
in featherbedding. It strikes me that in the real
world grown-ups have hard choices.

As Sonia pointed out in the young professionals focus
group, it's hard to be generous when you're working
brutal workweeks in a profession that creates a famine
on the time front. In her words, "anyone who gets a
break . . . is resented. So if you take reduced hours you
can expect to take a lot of heat. The only way around
this is for everyone to get a better deal."

7

HAVING IT ALL

"*D*ARN IT," SAID CINDY, 35, WHO lives in Raleigh, N.C., and is currently at home with her two children, Samantha, age four, and Sam, age seven.[1] "Men are always accusing me of being greedy when I say I want it all. But I'm not talking about bells and whistles. I'm talking about the basics: love and work. What sane person doesn't want that?

"I call it a crying shame that I was forced out of my career when Samantha was born because I wanted a reduced-hour schedule, and I've failed to find a way back in despite a bunch of fancy credentials. And it's not for want of trying. I've applied for dozens of jobs and I've networked like crazy, but no one seems interested in hiring an executive who wants to work 35–40 hours a week.

"Now maybe if I were shooting to be a *Fortune* 500 CEO I would expect to have to choose: career or children. But my game plan is to raise two kids and build a part-time career in middle management. Doesn't this sound reasonable?"

"I never meant not to have children," admitted Kate, 52, who is on the medical faculty at the University of Washington and lives in Seattle.[2]

> But I didn't finish my training until I was 35 and then I did a post-doc in Chicago. Looking back I can't think why I allowed my career to obliterate my thirties. I just didn't pay attention.
>
> I'm only just absorbing the consequences. I was looking at some data the other day and it hit me: If I reach age 65 in good health, the likelihood is I will live for another 19.1 years. That's an awfully long time to be on my own without the crutch of work. I don't know why it didn't occur to me before, but since I don't have children I also won't have grandchildren.

Cindy and Kate—both of whom participated in *High-Achieving Women, 2001*—represent different generations, belong to different professions, live in different parts of the country, and have chosen different life paths. Yet they share a powerful reality. Both feel they have been forced into unwanted choices: between career and family, and between love and work. The pain and regret in the voices of these women underscore a central theme of this book: the stunning scope—in terms of depth, breadth, and longevity—of the trade-offs that continue to haunt accomplished women. Only 16 percent of the respondents who participated in *High-Achieving Women, 2001* felt that it is very likely that a woman can "have it all." According to Harvard economist Claudia Goldin, this is almost precisely the percentage of women in the breakthrough generation who ended up with a career, a husband, and at least one child. In a 1995 study, Goldin found that only 13 to 17 percent of the women who graduated from college in the early 1970s achieved both career and a family.[3] These are small percentages. In terms of the fullness of women's lives, rather less has changed over the course of the last hundred years than we like to imagine. In 1897 Charlotte Perkins Gilman, the well-known feminist and activist, wrote:

> We have so arranged life that a man may have a
> house, a family, love, companionship, domesticity
> and fatherhood, yet remain an active citizen of age
> and country. We have so arranged life, on the
> other hand, that a woman must "choose"; she must
> either live alone, unloved, uncompanied, uncared

for, homeless, childless, with her work in the
world for sole consolation; or give up world service for the joys of love, motherhood and domestic
service.[4]

More than a century later, too many women are still
forced to make these difficult choices. Our survey tells
us that 42 percent of high-achieving women in corporate America are childless, and this figure rises to 49
percent among ultra-achievers. The vast majority of
these women did not choose to be childless; indeed, for
many, this "creeping nonchoice" is fraught with pain
and loss.

Our survey also tells us of the anguish—and waste—
involved in abandoning a career. *High-Achieving
Women, 2001* shows that fully two-thirds of high-
potential women who are not in careers feel they were
forced off the career highway and would like nothing
better than to find a way back on.

A large and growing body of research shows that
women are happiest when they are able to have both a
career and a family. Professional activity, it turns out,
provides mental stimulation, financial resources, self-
confidence, and adult friendship. When scholars compare the well-being of employed and nonemployed
mothers, they find a much higher level of satisfaction
and self-esteem—and less depression—among employed mothers than among nonemployed mothers,
and this finding holds up across a wide range of occu-

pations.[5] In her book *A Mother's Place,* journalist Susan Chira points out that women often see work as a form of power, mainly because it confers on them a precious degree of independence.[6] There is one important caveat, however: Mothers do much better in part-time or reduced-hour jobs. According to a 2000 study by University of Chicago sociologists Qin Chen and Ye Luo, mothers' experience of happiness is substantially related to the amount of time that they spend in paid employment.[7] Mothers who work long-hour jobs tend to be significantly less happy than mothers who work reduced-hour jobs, because 50- and 60-hour-a-week jobs heighten conflict between work and family.

Not surprisingly, working mothers are happier when they have enough leisure time to enjoy their children—to hang out at home, go to movies, play sports, visit museums and parks, travel together, share meals, and just talk. Chen and Luo came to the conclusion that part-time or reduced-hour careers "maximize" maternal well-being.[8]

If employment is good for women, so are marriage and children. In chapter 4 we examined powerful new evidence showing that marriage contributes to women's happiness. Well, there is a parallel body of evidence demonstrating that children greatly enhance the well-being of women.

In a series of books and articles that span more than a decade, University of Michigan sociologist Lois

Hoffman has examined the value of children to parents. Hoffman finds that across cultures parents see children as enormously important in warding off loneliness and providing love and companionship. In her research, mothers and fathers describe "the love children bring" and the fact that "you're never lonely" if you have children. She also stresses the ways in which parents see children as providing joy, stimulation, fun, and distraction: Mothers and fathers point to the fact that "there is always something going on" and that children "bring a liveliness to your life."[9]

Even more strikingly, children help parents deal with the central questions of human existence—how to find purpose beyond the self? How to cope with mortality? As Hoffman points out, these questions are particularly challenging "in urban, industrialized life where individuals feel less of an organic tie to the basic life processes."[10] Some people look to religion for help in answering these existential questions. Many more look to their children. Hoffman finds that children help parents satisfy the fundamental human need for meaning and purpose that transcends death.

To parents, children can confer a type of immortality. They are a link to the past, carrying on the genes of one's ancestors and the family name and traditions, but they are also a link to the future—a way of ensuring that one's characteristics and values, embodied in a dearly beloved child, live on after one is dead. Thus, children infuse the end of life with comfort and help mute its terror.

In a particularly important piece of research, Hoffman—with collaborators Karen McManus and Yvonne Brackbill—examined the lives of elderly parents and discovered that "the value of children is actualized in old age."[11] Fully three-quarters of elderly parents find their children to be a prime source of love, companionship, joy, and economic support. While few elderly parents take money from their children, almost half look to their children for protection against economic risk.

There is an impressive amount of contact between older parents and their children. According to Hoffman's study, 25 percent of elderly parents live within 15 miles of a child, and almost 40 percent have weekly contact with their children. Fewer than 3 percent of elderly parents see their children less than once a year. Kate's fear that she will sorely miss not having had children when she herself is elderly is amply borne out in this study.

The scholarship of Qin Chen, Lois Hoffman, and others provides an analytical and comparative framework for what many of us can figure out from our daily lives: If you are lucky enough to have both a career and a family, the odds are you will derive a great deal of happiness from both. And this is especially true over the long haul. As I know from personal experience, it's a great privilege to lead a life that encompasses both love and work.

At 6:30 A.M., one Friday last month, I headed off to La Guardia Airport to catch a flight to Greensboro, North Carolina—I had a speaking engagement in Winston-Salem. It was snowing and the plane needed to be de-iced—twice. As I sat in the plane I found myself becoming extremely nervous. There's nothing like waiting to take off in a snowstorm to pump up the anxiety level.

I have an exercise for such times. As my body tenses up, I close my eyes and conjure up an image of one of my children. Last Friday at La Guardia it was Adam—the younger of my two sons. The previous evening I had gone into his room at about 10:30 to say good night to him, but he had already fallen asleep, lying fully clothed on his bed, surrounded by an untidy mound of notes and books. European history had obviously done him in. I remembered lying down quietly by his side and nuzzling the delicate hollow in the nape of his neck. As I listened to his breathing, I felt the waves of my love washing over this sweetly gawky teenage boy, transforming both of us.

It always works. Conjuring up a tender scene with

one of my children eases the tension. My jaws unclench and I slowly release my white-knuckled grip on the arms of my seat. I gain a measure of serenity from knowing that if this wretched plane crashes, I will at least die in touch with the most powerful force I know about—my love for my children.

Of course, as soon as I arrived in North Carolina I was quickly reacquainted with why I get up at 5:30 on snowy mornings to catch flights to strange places thousands of miles away. I had been invited to Winston-Salem to give a keynote address at an event honoring Forsyth Family Focus—a countywide collaboration between family-support services and a group of local firms that include US Airways, RJ Reynolds, and Wachovia Bank. My task was to convince these companies that they need to provide many more benefits and services if working families are to flourish and thrive in their community.

As I stood behind the lectern at the Adam's Mark Winston Plaza Hotel facing 300 business executives, I knew I had a serious challenge on my hands. These were deeply conservative people who didn't believe in supporting working women or providing handouts for families.

But I'd done my homework. At this stage in the game I know how to inspire and cajole even an audience of recalcitrant businessmen. I used powerful local examples, emphasized a cost-benefit logic, and commended the companies that had made some headway on the work/family front. Soon the crowd was eating out of my hand. An hour later, as I basked in enthusiastic applause and foot stomping, I felt the thrill any professional feels when effectively plying his or her trade. Before I left Winston-Salem that afternoon, three companies asked me to help draft a list of family-friendly policies to include in their benefits package. Not bad, I thought, heading back to the airport for another anxious flight into snowbound La Guardia. Despite the inclement weather I was not staying over. I wanted to be home in time to put my three-year-old to bed.

The love I feel for my family is extraordinarily deep and the satisfaction I derive from my career is enormously real. Have they "cost" me? Dearly. Are they worth it? Every cent, every struggle. Should more women be able to choose both career and family? Absolutely.

Which brings us to the sixty-four-thousand-dollar question: Will this book help young women find both love and work? I think so.

The most important insights and strategies in these chapters focus on the individual. These clearly are the most helpful, for if you want to empower young women, you need to focus on what is immediately within their reach. To encapsulate exactly what women can do to enhance their chances of creating the lives they want, I've constructed a list.

1. Figure out what you want your life to look like at age 45. What do you want your personal life to look like? What do you want your career to look like? If it turns out that you want children (and approximately 86 percent of high-achieving women do) you need to become highly intentional—and seriously proactive. If you don't want children, the pressure is off.

2. Give urgent priority to finding a partner. This project is extremely time-sensitive and deserves special attention in your twenties. Understand that forging a loving, lasting marriage will enhance your life and make it much more likely that you will have children. The data presented in this book demonstrate that high-achieving women find it much easier to find partners at younger ages.

3. Have your first child before 35. The miracles of ART notwithstanding, do not wait until your late thirties or early forties before trying to have that first child. As we now understand, late-in-life childbearing is fraught with risk and failure. And even if you manage to get one child

"under the wire" you may fail to have a second. This, too, can trigger enormous regret.

4. Choose a career that will give you the "gift of time." Certain careers lend themselves to a better work/family balance because they provide more flexibility and are much more forgiving of career interruptions. As we now know, female entrepreneurs do much better than female lawyers in combining career and family. And lawyers do better than corporate women. Overall, there's a huge gap between entrepreneurs and executives in terms of how easily they're able to balance work and family. As Molly Friedrich pointed out in chapter 1, young women wanting both a career and children should think about avoiding professions with rigid career trajectories.

5. Choose a company that will help you achieve work/life balance. Companies vary widely in the kinds of work/life options they provide. If you are an ambitious young woman who wants a family, find a job at a firm that provides employees with a rich array of work/life policies that include reduced-hour schedules and various kinds of job-protected leave.

Thus, women can take a whole array of steps to guard against having to sacrifice either a career or a family. But identifying what an individual woman can do is only half the battle. The other half is convincing her that she is entitled to both a career and children. I mean, what will convince a woman that it's okay to get out and grab what she needs to make both happen?

First off, on a purely personal level, *the truth really does set you free*. To use the powerful words of Susan Chira, it is extraordinarily important that women "be given the freedom to make choices without being blinded and hounded by false debate . . . only then, unencumbered, can [women] make the decision that works best for them."[12] Knowing for a fact that only 3 percent of breakthrough generation women got married for the first time after age 35, and only 1 percent had a child after age 39, does serve to focus the mind and makes it easier to address the real-world compromises involved in actually getting married and having a child. It's also immensely helpful to know for a fact that women entrepreneurs do far better than corporate women in terms of balancing work and family, and that some employers really do allow employees to bend the rules. So, this onslaught of seemingly bleak facts and figures—many of them brand new—is profoundly liberating. These data can stiffen the backbone and spur action. In my interview with psychologist Bonnie

302 CREATING A LIFE

Maslin, she kept saying "if only": "If only women knew the facts; if only they were not blinded by hype and misinformation; if only they understood that if they wait they'll hit a wall."[13]

But while I hope the information in this book will help women make satisfying choices, I also hope it will help them make demands. This book pulls together data and analysis that, in their entirety, make a powerful case: Professional women have significant market power which they can use to stave off long workweeks and create more balanced lives.

Here is the argument in a nutshell: In today's information-based economy, education, skills, and experience are newly prized, and employers are beginning to realize that they cannot afford to lose large numbers of women professionals when they become mothers. Some of the more convincing arguments are spelled out in a 1999 study by McKinsey & Co. called *The War for Talent*.[14] This study, which surveyed 77 companies and 6,000 business executives, found that the most important corporate resource over the next 20 years will be human capital—specifically the education, skills, and experience embodied in talented professionals.[15] In the modern world, financial capital, infrastructural resources and cutting-edge technology are all readily available. Price might be a barrier but access is not an issue. Thus, human capital or "talent" has become the prime source of competitive advantage for companies around the world.

But if talent is the most important resource, it is also the one in shortest supply. In 15 years there will be 15 percent fewer Americans in the 35–45-year-old range than there are now. The McKinsey team predicted that for many companies, the search for the best and the brightest will become a constant, costly battle. Not only will companies have to devise more imaginative hiring practices; they will also have to work harder to keep their best people. According to the McKinsey team, "Today's high performers are like frogs in a wheelbarrow, they can jump out at any time."[16]

Of the 6,000 executives surveyed in the McKinsey study, 75 percent said they were chronically short of talent. Indeed, 40 percent of the companies surveyed said they were "talent constrained," in that they were unable to pursue growth opportunities because of a shortage of educated, skilled employees.

This point should not be overplayed, however. As we discovered earlier, the private sector is full of recalcitrant employers who either don't or won't understand the need to engage in a war for talent. It is also true that unforgiving career tracks and long workweeks are deeply entrenched in our corporate culture. In a recent interview, Maury Hanigan of the Hanigan Consulting Group expressed surprise that so few firms are even aware of the costs involved in losing talented employees.

> If a $2,000 desktop computer disappears from an employee's desk, I guarantee there'll be an investigation, a whole to-do. But if a $100,000 executive with all kinds of client relationships gets poached by a competitor—or quits to stay home with the kids—there's no investigation. No one is called on the carpet for it.[17]

Hanigan pointed out that only 40 percent of companies even keep tabs on turnover rates.

Despite these challenges I would like to stress that there is an important window of opportunity here. High-achieving women should take the information about talent wars and turnover costs and blast it from the rooftops. Employers need to be aware of these facts before they will even think about providing 30-hour-workweeks and other work/life options to accommodate working mothers. As we have seen, over the long haul most employers are dealing with a war for talent and need to figure out how to attract and retain professional women. In 2000, fully 22 percent of all women with professional degrees (MBAs and the like) were not in the labor market at all.[18] What an extraordinary waste of expensive talent! The private sector can ill afford to have almost a quarter of the highly qualified female talent pool forced out of their jobs when they have children.

This book also provides women with ammunition that might help spur government action—something that is long overdue in the United States. The fact is, the money, time, and love parents devote to their children benefit the rest of us, and our nation needs working women to become committed, effective parents.[19] Think about it for a minute. When a mother—or a father, for that matter—is able to devote the time and attention it takes for a child to grow into a well-adjusted person who succeeds in school and graduates from college, who benefits? Well, parents derive huge intangible rewards, among them love, companionship, and lifelong attachment. But the more concrete and tangible rewards go to the nation. Competent, well-developed children become productive workers who boost the GNP and pay their taxes. They also become responsible citizens who vote and otherwise contribute to society. Imagine the future of this country without a constantly replenished pool of capable, compassionate young people! Thus, we are all stakeholders in parents' ability to come through for their children. Government-sponsored family support initiatives like those described in chapter 6 can serve us all.

But I'm not holding my breath. As we understand from chapter 3, there is an impressive array of forces lined up against policies that support working mothers. They run the gamut from conservative ideologues who feel that government should not meddle in people's private lives, to the self-described "childfree" who resent parent perks. Disparate though its sources are, resistance is fierce and deep.

But if widespread public support for working parents is some way off, it is not too soon to make this link to national interest. If there were a wider appreciation for motherhood in society, women might quit apologizing for wanting both a career and a family, and hold their heads high when going to the boss and asking for a reduced-hour work schedule.

Just remember: When a woman has a child, she is not indulging an expensive hobby; rather, she is taking on an awesome responsibility that has serious societal significance. She is therefore entitled to some support. Having it all, it turns out, is a good idea—for individual women and for the nation.

NOTES

Preface to the Original Edition

1. Some of the initial interviews were done with my long-time friend and coauthor, Cornel West.

2. The survey was fielded in partnership with the National Parenting Association and Harris Interactive. For further details, see chapter 2.

3. Interview with author, December 15, 2000.

4. Interview with author, July 25, 2001.

5. Ellen Galinsky, keynote address, WorkLife Congress 2001 sponsored by *Working Mother* magazine, New York, October 10, 2001.

Chapter 1

1. In 1998 19 percent of American women were childless at ages 40–44. Thus the rate of childlessness among high-achieving women is roughly twice the rate in the population at large. Overall rates of childlessness have increased in recent years. See: U.S. Census Bureau, "Fertility of American Women," Washington, D.C., September, 2000.

2. *High-Achieving Women, 2001.* New York: National Parenting Association, April 2002.

3. *The New York Times,* December 23, 1999.

4. Interview with author, January 13, 1999.

5. Interview with author, January 13, 1999.

6. *High-Achieving Women, 2001.*

7. Interviews with author, September 14 and September 19, 2000.

8. Interview with author, November 21, 2000.

9. Interview with author, March 10, 2000.

10. Wendy Wasserstein, *The Heidi Chronicles*. New York: Harcourt Brace Jovanovich, 1990, p. 21.

11. Interview with the author, December 5, 2000.

12. Names and affiliations have been changed.

13. Interview with author, February 28, 2000. Names and affiliations have been changed.

14. Interview with author, December 5, 2000.

15. Interview with author, February 25, 2000.

16. Interview with author, April 30, 2001.

17. Wendy Wasserstein, *An American Daughter*. New York: Harcourt, Brace & Co., 1998, p. 81.

Chapter 2

1. The survey included a nationally representative sample of 1186 high-achieving career women aged 28–55 years, a nationally representative sample of 479 high-achieving non-career women aged 28–55, and a nationally representative sample of 472 high-achieving men aged 28–55. The survey was self-administered on-line through the Internet.

High-achieving career women are defined as women who are employed full-time or self-employed and earn an income that places them in the top 10 percent of their age group (at least $55,000 per year for women 28–40 and at least $65,000 per year for women 41–55 years old), or women who have a doctorate or who have a professional degree in medicine, law, or dentistry. The sample includes an oversample of "ultra" high-achieving career women earning at least $100,000— which places them in the top 1 percent of their age group.

High-achieving noncareer women are defined as women

who are highly educated but not currently in full-time employment. They have completed a bachelor's degree with high honors, or completed graduate school/professional school, or obtained a CPA qualification. Either they are out of the labor market completely, or they are at work only a small number of hours a week. In the text these women are often referred to as *high-potential women.*

High-achieving career men are defined as men who are employed full-time or self-employed and earn an income that places them in the top 10 percent of their age group (at least $80,000 for men 28–40 years old and at least $95,000 for men 41–55 years old), or who have completed graduate school/professional school.

The interviews averaged 17 minutes in length and were conducted between January 5, 2001, and January 12, 2001.

The survey was carried out by Harris Interactive under the auspices of the National Parenting Association, a non-profit research organization. Funding for the survey and the associated research was provided by Ernst & Young, Merck Inc., The Annie E. Casey Foundation and the David and Lucile Packard Foundation.

For details of the methodology and findings see: *High-Achieving Women, 2001.* New York: National Parenting Association, April, 2002. See also www.parentsunite.org. It should be noted that Norma Vite-León of the Economics department at New School University performed additional calculations using data from the *High-Achieving Women, 2001* survey.

2. According to the definition used in *High-Achieving Women, 2001,* corporate America includes all companies with more than 5,000 employees.

3. It should be noted that in the category of ultra-achieving men the sample size is small and results should be interpreted cautiously.

4. This 14 percent figure for high-achieving women is a little higher than in the female population at large. Across income groups and across countries, approximately 9–12 percent of young women state that they expect to remain childless. In 1992 the Census Bureau found that 9 percent of American women plan to remain childless. This is the last year these data were collected. Interview with Martin O'Connell, Fertility Division, U.S. Census Bureau, November 28, 2001. A recent study in the United Kingdom finds that 10 percent of young British women plan to remain childless, while in Australia the figure is 11 percent. See: Fiona McAllister, "Choosing Childlessness," Family Policy Studies Centre, London, July 1998, and "Reasons for People's Decisions Not to Have Children," Australian Institute of Family Studies, Melbourne, May 2001.

5. These figures are appreciably lower than in the population at large. Nationwide, 67 percent of women aged 40–44 years are currently married. See U.S. Census Bureau, "Current Population Report," June 2001.

6. It should also be noted that in the category of African-American women the sample size is small and results should be interpreted cautiously.

7. Figures calculated by Norma Vite-León from *High-Achieving Women, 2001* data.

8. A 1986 study by Heidrick and Struggles examined the lives of high-achieving women across a range of careers and found that 54 percent of these women were childless. See Felice N. Schwartz and Jean Zimmerman, *Breaking with*

Tradition: Women and Work, the New Facts of Life. New York: Warner Books, 1992.

In a 1993 book, Deborah Swiss and Judith Walker explored the challenges facing female graduates of Harvard's professional schools when they attempted to combine career and family. They found that 34 percent of these women were childless. See Deborah J. Swiss and Judith P. Walker, *Women and the Work/Family Dilemma: How Today's Professional·Women are Finding Solutions*, 1993.

A 1994 article by Ellen Fagenson and Janice Jackson, which examined the lives of American business managers, found that 61 percent of women executives were childless. See Ellen A. Fagenson and Janice J. Jackson, "The Status of Women Managers in the United States," in Nancy J. Adler and Dafna N. Israeli, eds., *Competitive Frontiers: Women Managers in a Global Economy*. Oxford: Blackwell, 1994.

A 1996 study of women in corporate leadership by Catalyst found that 36 percent of these women were childless. See *Women in Corporate Leadership: Progress and Prospects*, Catalyst, 1996.

A 1998 study of women in academe found that 50 percent of university women were childless. See Regina M. Watkins, Margie Herrin, and Lonnie R. McDonald, "The Juxtaposition of Career and Family: A Dilemma for Professional Women," Advancing Women in Leadership, Winter 1998.

A 2001 study of women on Wall Street found that only half of the women surveyed had children compared to three-quarters of the men. In the words of this study, many women are being forced to make "significant sacrifices in their personal lives." See "Women in Financial Services: The Word on the Street," Catalyst, July 25, 2001.

9. Claudia Goldin, "Career and Family: College Women Look to the Past." Cambridge Mass.: National Bureau of Economic Research, Working Paper No. 5188, 1995.

10. See : Danity Little, *How Women Executives Succeed: Lessons and Experiences from the Federal Government.* Westport, Conn.: Quorum Books, 1994; Deborah Swiss, *Women Breaking Through: Overcoming the Final 10 Obstacles at Work.* Princeton, N.J.: Pacesetter Books, 1996; and *Women and the MBA: Gateway to Opportunity*, Catalyst, 2000.

11. If Marilyn feels overloaded, she is not alone. A recent study by the Families and Work Institute finds that nearly a third of U.S. employees often or very often feel overworked or overwhelmed by how much work they have to do. See: "Feeling Overworked: When Work Becomes Too Much," Families and Work Institute, May 2001.

12. According to *High-Achieving Women, 2001,* when neither spouse takes prime responsibility for a house-related or child-related task, it is either shared between the spouses or not done at all.

13. U.S. Census Bureau, "Current Population Survey," March 2000.

Chapter 3

1. Interviews with author May 5 and November 1, 2000.

2. Felice N. Schwartz and Jean Zimmerman, *Breaking with Tradition: Women and Work, the New Facts of Life.* New York: Warner Books, 1992, p. 67.

3. Interview with author, December 20, 2000.

4. Jane Waldfogel, "The Effects of Children on Women's Wages," *American Sociology Review*, vol. 62, 1997, pp. 209–217; and Michelle J. Budig and Paula England, "The

Wage Penalty for Motherhood," *American Sociological Review*, vol. 66, 2001, pp. 201–225.

5. Interview with author, September 23, 2000.

6. U.S. Department of Labor, Bureau of Labor Statistics, "Employment and Earnings," January 2000. Despite this impressive trendline, it's important not to overstate the gains of women. Recent studies show that more than half of the shrinking wage gap is due to a fall in the real wages of men. Less than 50 percent is a result of women being paid more. See Heidi Hartmann and Julie Whittaker, "Stall in Women's Real Wages Slows Progress in Closing the Wage Gap," Research-in-brief, Institute for Women's Policy Research, February 1998. Figures updated.

7. Current Population Survey, *Bureau of Labor Statistics,* 2001.

8. Catalyst press release, November 13, 2000.

9. Catalyst press release, November 11, 1999.

10. American Bar Association, "A Snapshot of Women in the Law in the Year 2000," http://www.abanet.org/women/snapshots.pdf, accessed September 25, 2001.

11. Cited in Sylvia Ann Hewlett, *A Lesser Life*. New York: William Morrow, 1986, p. 85

12. Susan Harkness and Jane Waldfogel, "The Family Gap in Pay: Evidence from Seven Industrialised Countries," Centre for Analysis of Social Exclusion, London School of Economics, November 1999, p. 21. This study calculates the mean hourly wages of women as a percentage of the mean hourly wages of men. See also Francine D. Blau and Lawrence M. Kahn, "Wage Structure and Gender Earnings Differentials: an International Comparison," *Economica*, 1996, 63, pp. 29–62.

13. Interview with Jane Waldfogel, July 17, 2001. See also

Susan Harkness and Jane Waldfogel, "The Family Gap in Pay," Table 3.

14. Lester C. Thurow, "63 Cents to the Dollar: The Earnings Gap Doesn't Go Away," *Working Mother,* October, 1984, p. 42.

15. Interview with author, October 26, 2000.

16. Interview with author, June 15, 2001. See also Jane Waldfogel, "Understanding the 'Family Gap' in Pay for Women with Children," *Journal of Economic Perspectives,* vol. 12, no. 1, Winter 1998: p. 143.

17. Linda J. Waite and Maggie Gallagher, *The Case for Marriage: Why Married People are Happier, Healthier, and Better off Financially.* New York: Doubleday, 2000, p. 99.

18. Waldfogel, "Understanding the 'Family Gap' in Pay for Women with Children," p. 145.

19. Solomon William Polachek, "Women in the Economy: Perspectives on Gender Inequality." Paper presented at the U.S. Commission on Civil Rights Conference on Comparative Worth, June 6, 1984.

20. Survey entitled "Value of a Mum" carried out in 2000 by Legal & General. See discussion in "Housework Still Done by Women," *Guardian,* March 10, 2000. According to this survey, full-time working mothers spend 56 hours a week on domestic labor, part-time working mothers 68 hours, and housewives put in 76 hours.

21. This finding reinforces the results of a recent study that demonstrates that instead of having someone to share the work with, marriage causes housework to increase significantly for women. Married women perform 14 hours more housework each week than single women. By way of contrast, married men perform only 90 minutes more. See Chloe E. Bird, "Gender,

Household Labor and Psychological Distress: The Impact of the Amount and Division of Housework," *Journal of Health and Social Behavior,* vol. 40, March 2001, pp. 32–45.

22. Nora Ephron, *Heartburn.* New York: Pocket Books, 1983, p. 104.

23. Scott Coltrane, "Research on Household Labor: Modeling and Measuring the Social Embeddedness of Routine Family Work," *Journal of Marriage and the Family,* vol. 62, November 2000, pp. 1208–1233. This article reviews more than 200 scholarly articles and books on household labor published between 1989 and 1999.

24. Susan Harkness and Jane Waldfogel, "The Family Gap in Pay: Evidence from Seven Industrialised Countries," op. cit., pp. 9–10.

25. John Carvel, "Britain's Childcare Worst in Europe," *Guardian,* September 3, 2001.

26. Heather Joshi, Pierella Paci, and Jane Waldfogel, "The Wages of Motherhood: Better or Worse?" *Cambridge Journal of Economics,* vol. 1999, pp. 543–564. It's important to point out that even when a new mother is supported with paid maternity/parenting leave and maintains a continuous work history, she still earns less than women without children. Comparing women with similar work histories, Waldfogel found that one child still reduces a woman's lifetime earnings by 4 percent. See Jane Waldfogel, "The Effect of Children on Women's Wages," *American Sociology Review,* vol. 62, 1997, pp. 209–217.

27. See discussion in Dolores Hayden, *The Grand Domestic Revolution.* Cambridge, Mass.: MIT Press, 1981. See also Charlotte Perkins Gilman, *Concerning Children.* Boston: Small, Maynard & Co., 1901; and Charlotte Perkins

Gilman, *The Living of Charlotte Perkins Gilman.* New York: Harper & Row, 1975, p. 163.

28. Interview with author, September 20, 1996. See also Edward N. Wolff, "The Economic Status of Parents in Postwar America," in Sylvia Ann Hewlett, Nancy Rankin, and Cornel West, eds., *Taking Parenting Public: The Case for a New Social Movement.* Lanham, MD: Rowman & Littlefield, 2002.

29. See discussion in Sylvia Ann Hewlett and Cornel West, *The War Against Parents.* Boston: Houghton Mifflin Co., 1998, pp. 88–124.

30. Interview with author, May 31, 2000.

Chapter 4

1. Interview with author, September 13, 2000.

2. Helen Fielding, *Bridget Jones's Diary.* London: Penguin Books, 1996.

3. "The Marriage Crunch," *Newsweek*, June 2, 1986, p. 54.

4. Interview with author, October 17, 2000.

5. U.S. Census Bureau, "Current Population Survey," March Supplement, 2000.

6. David Brooks, *Bobos in Paradise.* New York: Simon and Schuster, 2000, p. 15.

7. Interview with author, September 23, 2000.

8. Interview with author, February 3, 2001.

9. Interview with author, January 23, 2001.

10. Interview with author, October 17, 2000.

11. *Hooking Up, Hanging Out and Hoping for Mr. Right: College Women on Mating and Dating Today.* New York: Institute for American Values, July 2001.

12. Interview with author, January 26, 2001.

13. Jessie Bernard, *The Future of Marriage*. New Haven, Conn.: Yale University Press, 1982, p. 14.

14. Ibid., p. 51.

15. Betty Friedan, *The Feminine Mystique*. New York: Dell Publishing, 1963, p. 256.

16. Ibid., p. 203

17. Much of this new research is pulled together in a book by Waite and Gallagher. See Linda J. Waite and Maggie Gallagher, *The Case for Marriage: Why Married People Are Happier, Healthier and Better Off Financially*. New York: Doubleday, 2000.

18. Allan V. Horwitz, Helene Raskin White, and Sandra Howell-White, "Becoming Married and Mental Health: A Longitudinal Study of a Cohort of Young Adults," *Journal of Marriage and the Family*, vol. 58, 1996, pp. 895–907. It should be noted that this study controlled for premarital rates of mental health—to eliminate the possibility that a relationship between marital status and well-being exists only because healthier individuals tend to be the ones that get married.

19. David G. Blanchflower and Andrew J. Oswald, "Well-being over time in Britain and the USA," Working Paper 7487, National Bureau of Economic Research, Cambridge, Mass., January 2000.

20. Lupton and Smith found that over a five-year period, married couples saved $11,000–$14,000 more than nonmarried households. See Joseph Lupton and James P. Smith, "Marriage, Assets, and Savings," RAND, Labor and Population Program, Working Paper 99–12, November 1999, p.20. See also Waite and Gallagher, *The Case For Marriage*, op. cit., pp. 97–124.

21. Laurence J. Kotlikoff and Avia Spivak, "The Family As an Incomplete Annuities Market," *Journal of Political Economy*, vol. 89, 1981, pp. 372–391.

22. All figures cited in this paragraph are taken from "The National Health and Social Life Survey," carried out in 1992 at the University of Chicago by Edward Laumann, John Gagnon, Robert Michael, and Stuart Michaels. This survey is popularly known as "The National Sex Survey."

23. Interview with author, November 15, 2000.

24. Interview with author, January 23, 2001.

Chapter 5

1. Interview with author, March 28, 2000.

2. Interview with author, September 12, 2000. See also Anne Newman, "The Risks of Racing the Reproductive Clock," *BusinessWeek*, May 5, 1997.

3. In 1968 for example, 3,790 babies were born to women aged 45–49. See: National Center for Health Statistics, National Vital Statistics Report, "Births: Final Data for 1998," March 2000, p. 6.

4. *People*, June 9, 2000.

5. Susan Cheever, "A New York Fable," *Talk*, February 2000.

6. Hallie Levine, "Older Women Weigh Pregnancy Perils," *New York Post*, July 16, 2000.

7. Interview with author, September 17, 2000.

8. Raphael Ron-El, Arie Raziel, Devorah Strassburger, Morey Schachter, Ester Kasterstein, and Shevach Friedler, "Outcome of Assisted Reproductive Technology in Women over the Age of 41," *Fertility and Sterility*, September 2000, vol. 74, no. 3, pp. 471–475.

9. A. Anderson, J. Wohlfahrt, et al., "Maternal Age and Fetal Loss: Population Based Register Linkage Study," *British Medical Journal,* 2000, pp. 1708–1712.

10. Quoted in Richard Marrs, *Fertility Book: America's Leading Fertility Expert Tells You Everything You Need to Know About Getting Pregnant.* New York: Delacorte Press, 1997, p. 48.

11. Anne Adams Lang, "Doctors Are Second Guessing the 'Miracle' of Multiple Births," *The New York Times,* June 13, 1999.

12. Pam Belluck, "Heartache Frequently Visits Parents with Multiple Births," *The New York Times,* January 3, 1998.

13. Sarog Saigal, Lorraine A. Hoult, David L. Streiner, Barbara L. Stoskopf, and Peter L. Rosenbaum, "School Difficulties at Adolescence in a Regional Cohort of Children Who Were Extremely Low Birth Weight," *Pediatrics*, vol. 105, no. 2, February 2000.

14. Sheryl Gay Stolberg, "As the Tiniest Babies Grow: So Can Their Problems," *The New York Times*, May 8, 2000.

15. Marrs, *Fertility Book,* op. cit., p. 46.

16. Alice S. Whittemore, Robin Harris, and Jacqueline Itnyre, "Characteristics Relating to Ovarian Cancer Risk: Collaborative Analysis of 12 U.S. Case-Control Studies," *American Journal of Epidemiology*, November 15, 1992, vol. 136, no. 10, pp. 1184–1203.

17. Mary Anne Rossing, J.R. Daling, N.S. Weiss, D.E. Moore, and S.G. Self, "Ovarian Tumors in a Cohort of Infertile Women," *New England Journal of Medicine,* vol. 331, no. 12, September 22, 1994, pp. 771–776.

18. Alison Venn, Lyndsey Watson, Fiona Bruinsma,

Graham Giles, and David Healy, "Risk of Cancer after Use of Fertility Drugs with In-Vitro Fertilization," *The Lancet*, vol. 354, November 6, 1999, pp. 1586–1590.

19. Gad Potashnik, Liat Lerner-Geva, Leonid Genkin, Angela Chetrit, Eitan Lunenfeld, and Avi Porath, "Fertility Drugs and the Risk of Breast and Ovarian Cancers: Results of a Long-Term Follow-up Study," *Fertility and Sterility*, vol. 71, no. 5, May 1999.

20. Asher Shushan and Neri Laufer, "Fertility Drugs and Ovarian Cancer: What Are the Practical Implications of the Ongoing Debate?" *Fertility and Sterility*, vol. 74, no. 1., July 2000.

21. Liz Tilberis, *No Time to Die*. New York: Avon Books, 1998, p. 235.

22. Anne Adams Lang, op. cit.

23. Infertility treatment often creates intense economic pressure. The Incid website is full of stories of financial stress. E.g., Tracy Bailey tells of the toll taken by five years of unsuccessful infertility treatment. In her words, "you pay as much if you lose a baby as if you deliver one. I generally try to miscarry at home so as to save money. And then I try to catch what I can in the toilet bowl so that it can be tested." http://www.incid.org.

24. Anne Adams Lang, op. cit.

25. The United Kingdom seems to be particularly strict. In a recent, much-publicized case, a 46-year-old woman wanted to have more than three embryos implanted to increase her chances of getting pregnant and sought a review by the courts of the HFEA guidelines, which limit transfers to three. She was turned down. The reason given was the risk of multiple births.

26. Laurent Belsie, "Multiple Births Stir Call for Controls

on Fertility," *Christian Science Monitor*, December 28, 1998.

27. Richard Marrs, op. cit., p. 41.

28. Rick Lyman, "As Octuplets Remain in Peril, Ethics Questions Are Raised," *The New York Times,* December 22, 1998.

29. Dr. Alan Tounson, an embryologist at Monash University in Melbourne, Australia, pioneered the use of donor eggs in 1984. See Rebecca Mead, "Eggs for Sale," *The New Yorker,* August 9, 1999.

30. http://www.ronsangels.com/auction.html.

31. Interview with author, March 10, 2000.

32. Deanne Corbett, "Science: Making a Baby," *The Stanford Daily,* March 10, 1999.

33. Richard Marrs, op. cit., p. 137.

34. Richard Marrs, op. cit., p. 136.

35. The Emily story was featured on NPR's *Morning Edition*, December 23, 1998. Transcript # 98122306-210

36. Gina Kolata, "Price of Donor Eggs Soars, Setting Off a Debate on Ethics," *The New York Times*, February 25, 1998.

37. K.K. Ahudja and E.G. Simons, "Cancer of the Colon in an Egg Donor: Policy Repercussions for Donor Recruitment," *Human Reproduction,* vol. 13, no. 1, 1998, pp. 227–223. See also Margarette Driscoll, "Birth of Doubt," *Sunday Times*, March 15, 1998.

38. Sauer, Paulson, and Lobo, 1995, p. 114. Cited in Marrs, *Fertility Book,* p. 134.

39. Quoted in Marrs, *Fertility Book*, op. cit., p. 137.

40. Claudia Kalb, "The Truth About Fertility." *Newsweek,* August 13, 2001.

41. Address to conference hosted by RESOLVE NYC,

"Everything You Ever Wanted to Know about Infertility and Adoption," Mt. Sinai Hospital, New York, September 17, 2000. See also Zev Rosenwaks, "We Still Can't Stop the Biological Clock," *The New York Times,* June 24, 2000.

42. Genesis 30:22-23.

43. Barbara Grizzuti Harrison, "Men Don't Know Nuthin' 'Bout Birthin' Babies," *Esquire,* July 1972, p. 110.

44. Edward Shorter, *Women's Bodies: A Social History of Women's Encounter with Health, Ill-Health and Medicine.*New York: Transaction Publishers, 1991, p. 31.

45. Ibid., p. 31.

46. Harold Speert, *Essays in Eponymy: Obstetric and Gynecologic Milestones.* New York: Macmillan, 1958, pp. 442–443.

47. W.J. Sinclair, "The Injuries of Parturition: The Old and the New," *British Medical Journal,* September 4, 1987, pp. 589–595.

48. Edward Shorter, *Women's Bodies,* p. 272.

49. Uta Ranke-Heinemann, *Eunuchs for the Kingdom of Heaven: Women, Sexuality and the Catholic Church.* New York: Penguin Books, 1990, pp. 25–26.

Chapter 6

1. Focus group, Cambridge, Massachusetts, February 12, 2001. Names and affiliations have been changed.

2. The vignettes contained in this chapter are based on follow-up interviews with respondents to the *High-Achieving Women, 2001* survey. Names and other identifying information have been changed. See description of survey in Chapter 2.

3. Juliet B. Schor, *The Overworked American: The Unexpected Decline of Leisure.* New York: Basic Books,

1992; Arlie Hochschild, *The Time Bind: When Work Becomes Home and Home Becomes Work*. New York: Henry Holt & Co., 1997.

4. See Jerry A. Jacobs and Kathleen Gerson, "Do Americans Feel Overworked? Comparing Ideal and Actual Working Time," in Toby Parcel and Daniel B. Cornfield, eds., *Work and Family: Research Informing Policy*. Thousand Oaks, Calif.: Sage Publications, 1998. See also Juliet B. Schor, "Time Crunch among American Parents," in Sylvia Ann Hewlett, Nancy Rankin, and Cornel West, eds. *Taking Parenting Public: The Case for a New Social Movement*. Lanham, Md.: Rowman and Littlefield, 2002.

5. The picture is, of course, complicated by the fact that individuals often need to hold more than one of these part time jobs to get by. Jody Heymann describes these trends and points to the consequences. See: Jody Heymann, MD, PhD, *The Widening Gap: Why America's Working Families Are in Jeopardy and What Can Be Done about It*. New York: Basic Books, 2000.

6. Jerry A. Jacobs and Kathleen Gerson, "Towards a Family-Friendly, Gender Equitable Work Week," *University of Pennsylvania Journal of Labor and Employment Law*, Fall 1998, pp. 458–459.

7. See discussion in Paula M. Rayman, *Beyond the Bottom Line*. St. Martin's Press, 2001, pp. 25–59.

8. Pamela Holloway, "The Financial Impact of the War for Talent," http://www.thepepeoplepractice.com. See also pam@aboutpeople.com. Accessed December 4, 2001.

9. University of Texas, Houston, "Work/Family Task Force Report," May 1996. http://oac.uth.tmc.edu/family/wftaskforce.html.

10. "Friends of the Family," *Working Mother,* October 2000, p. 62.

11. B. Lynn Ware and Bruce Fern, "The Challenge of Retaining Top Talent: The Workforce Attrition Crisis," Integral Training Systems, Inc., 1997. http://www.itsinc.net/retention-research.htm. See also, John Sullivan, "The Cost Factors and Business Impacts of Turnover," March 1998. http://ourworld.compuserve.com/homepages/gately/pp15js10.htm.

12. American Management Association, "2000 AMA Staffing & Structure Survey," October 2000, p. 1.

13. Interview with author, September 11, 2001.

14. Darrell Rigby, "Moving Upward in a Downturn," *Harvard Business Review,* June 2001, pp. 99–105.

15. Interview with author, December 20, 2000.

16. According to *Working Mother* magazine, the ten best companies are: Allstate Insurance Company, Bank of America, Eli Lily and Company, Fannie Mae, IBM Corporation, Life Technologies, Inc., Lincoln Financial Group, Merrill Lynch & Co., Inc, Novant Health Inc., and Prudential. See *Working Mother,* "100 Best Companies for Working Mothers, October 2000, pp. 76–84.

17. Options available at Ernst & Young (21,842 employees) include: *flexible hours,* which allow employees to work irregular hours, compressed workweeks, or reduced days during less busy times, balanced by longer days during more busy times; *reduced schedules,* which allow employees to work fewer days per week and fewer hours per day; and *seasonal long-term arrangements,* which allow employees to work a normal work schedule for most of the year, followed by a period of time off that can last from two weeks to three

months. Source: http://www.diversityinc.com/workforce/
wlife/eyworklife.

Flexible work arrangements are already affecting turnover
rates at Ernst & Young. According to Deborah Holmes,
Americas Director, Center for the New Workforce, "Two-
thirds of the people using flexible work arrangements tell us
that they would have left—or would not have joined us in the
first place—if it had not been for their flexible work arrangement." Source: Interview with author, October 17, 2000.

Since 1991, IBM (143,399 employees) has offered a three-
year *personal leave of absence* for full-time employees (see
interview with Amy). This leave is unpaid but benefits are continued and there are job-back guarantees. Since 1997, unpaid
leave has been supplemented by part-time paid leave—IBM
calls this option *flexible leave of absence*. Employees who take
this leave work a minimum of 16 hours a week for up to three
years, and receive prorated pay and vacation, full benefits, and
the opportunity to earn pay increases and bonuses.

Senior managers at IBM feel that creative work/life policies have helped attract and retain high-caliber women
workers. Twenty-one percent of executive employees at IBM
are now women, up from 12 percent in 1995. "Our motiva-
tion is not to be generous, but to be astute in the management of our human resource talent pool," said Ted Childs,
vice president of global workforce diversity at IBM. Source:
http://www.workingwoman.com, accessed February 20, 2001.

Merck & Co., Inc. (32,722 employees) offers 26 weeks of
family leave—with partial pay and phaseback options for
new mothers. The company also contributes to the operating
costs of three on-site childcare centers and provides subsidies
and discounts for use at community childcare centers.

Women now account for half of Merck's research scientists and 36 percent of top earners in the company—much higher figures than for the pharmaceutical industry as a whole. Source: http://www.workingwoman.com, accessed February 20, 2001.

Scholastic Corporation (1,800 employees at headquarters) has developed what it calls "a culture of flexibility." Take for example Scholastic's *family leave plan,* which predates FMLA. For employees who have been at the company for at least one year, Scholastic provides maternity leave at full pay for 4 to 26 weeks—depending on how many years the employee has been with the company. The company also provides *child care leave*—eight weeks of fully paid leave for the primary caregiver following maternity leave or upon adoption. A secondary care parent is entitled to two weeks fully paid leave following birth or adoption. In addition, to ease the transition back to work, a primary caregiver who has just taken eight weeks of childcare leave will receive full salary for part-time work for an additional eight weeks—assuming they put in at least 21 hours per week at the office. Source: Interview, Deborah Fuller, Director of Human Resources, Scholastic, June 18, 2001.

18. Chart 1 ACCESS TO WORK/LIFE POLICIES

	High-achieving Career Women	High-achieving Non-Career Women (Not currently employed)
	%	%
Change starting and quitting times on a flexible basis	69 percent	49 percent
Return to work gradually after childbirth/adoption	56 percent	39 percent

Work at home or off-site on a regular basis	48 percent	28	percent
Paid time off for female employees who give birth to a child	46 percent	37	percent
Compress their workweek	42 percent	28	percent
Share jobs	31 percent	28	percent
Paid time off for male employees whose partner gives birth to a child	29 percent	19	percent
Childcare at or near work	20 percent	14	percent
Tale a "career break"	12 percent	8	percent

Source: *High-Achieving Women, 2001*

19. Keith H. Hammonds, "Family Values," *Fast Company,* December 2000, p. 170. DeGroot makes the point that even a generous package of benefits cannot help employees strike a meaningful, sustainable balance between professional and personal life unless there is a fundamental change in the mind-set of managers. See also Stewart D. Friedman, Perry Christensen, and Jessica DeGroot, "Work and Life: The End of the Zero-Sum Game," *Harvard Business Review,* Nov.–Dec., 1998.

20. Jacobs and Gerson, op. cit., p. 462

21. http://www.lawyerslifecoach.com/newsletters/issueso8, accessed January 7, 2001.

22. It is worth pointing out that Schwartz herself never used the term "Mommy Track." Instead she talked about "career primary women" and "career and family women." See: Felice N. Schwartz, "Management Women and the New Facts of Life," *Harvard Business Review,* Jan.–Feb. 1989, pp. 65–76.

23. See discussion in Ann Crittenden, *The Price of Motherhood*. New York: Henry Holt, 2001, p. 32.

24. Rhona Mahony, *Kidding Ourselves*. New York: Basic Books, 1995, p. 18.

25. Nancy Rankin, "Leave-Taking Employees Need 'On-Ramps'," *Human Resources Report*, vol. 19 no. 43, November 6, 2000, p. 1181.

26. There are currently a slew of legislative proposals at both the state and federal levels—spearheaded by the National Partnership for Families and Children—that would accomplish the objective of creating paid family leave. See: http://www.nationalpartnership.org/workand family/fmleave/flinsur.htm.

27. See discussion in Stanley I. Greenspan, *The Four-Thirds Solution: Solving the Child-Care Crisis in America Today*. Cambridge Mass.: Perseus Publishing, 2001.

Chapter 7

1. Not her real name, survey respondent from *High-Achieving Women, 2001*.

2. Ibid.

3. Claudia Goldin, "Career and Family: College Women Look to the Past," Cambridge Mass., National Bureau of Economic Research, 1995, Working Paper No. 5188.

4. Dolores Hayden, *The Grand Domestic Revolution*. Cambridge, Mass.: MIT Press, 1981, p. 197.

5. See, for example, C.E. Ross and J. Mirowsky, "Does Employment Affect Health?" *Journal of Health and Social Behavior,* vol. 36, 1995, pp. 230–243; and M.M. Ferre, "Beyond Separate Spheres: Feminism and Family Research," *Journal of Marriage and the Family,* vol. 52, 1990, pp. 866–884.

6. Susan Chira, *A Mother's Place: Choosing Work and Family Without Guilt or Blame.* New York: HarperCollins, 1998, p. 151.

7. Qin Chen and Ye Luo, "What Matters More, Jobs or Children? A Study of Time Use and Experience of Happiness among Dual-Earner Couples," Sloan Center, University of Chicago, working paper, August 2000.

8. Ibid., p.15.

9. Lois Wladis Hoffman and Jean Denby Manis, "The Value of Children in the United States: A New Approach to the Study of Fertility," *Journal of Marriage and the Family*, August 1979, p. 583.

10. Ibid., p. 587.

11. Lois Wladis Hoffman, Karen Ann McManus, and Yvonne Brackbill, "The Value of Children to Young and Elderly Parents," *International Journal of Aging and Human Development,*" vol. 25, no. 4, 1987.

12. Susan Chira, *A Mother's Place,* op. cit., p. 282.

13. Interview with author, January 23, 2001.

14. Elizabeth G. Chambers, Mark Foulon, Helen Handfield-Jones, Steven M. Hankin, and Edward G. Michaels, "The War for Talent," *The McKinsey Quarterly,* 1998, p. 3.

15. Ibid.

16. http://www.mckinsey.com/features/frogs/index.html.

17. Interview with author, May 30, 2001.

18. U.S. Census Bureau, 2001.

19. According to economist Nancy Folbre, Americans have a hard time seeing children as public goods, rather than tend to think of children as pets. See Nancy Folbre, *The Invisible Heart: Economics and Family Values.* New York: The New Press, 2001, p. 109.